ITALY

Jewish Travel Guide

Annie Sacerdoti & Luca Fiorentino

Translated by Richard F. De Lossa

Edited and designed by Oscar Israelowitz

ISRAELOWITZ PUBLISHING
P.O.Box 228 Brooklyn, NY 11229
Tel. (718) 951-7072
E-Mail oscari 477 @aol.com

With permission from Casa Editrice Marietti S.p.A - Casale Monferrato
Sede Centrale: Via Adam 19 15033 Casale Monferrato (AL) Tel. (0142) 76311

Library of Congress Catalog Card Number: 99-83965
International Standard Book Number: 1-878741-42-X

Printed in the United States.

Cover Photo:
Synagogue of Vittorio Veneto (1702), presently located in the Israel Museum, Jerusalem. (Photo Courtesy of Israel Museum/David Harris)

Printed by MORIAH OFFSET CO. 718-693-3800

CONTENTS

AUTHOR'S PREMISE

Three Years ago, RAI 3 Television asked me to work on a documentary about the history of the Jews in the Lombardy region of Italy. It was on that occasion that I discovered the synagogue of Rivarolo Mantovano with a portrait of Garibaldi in place of the Holy Ark, the synagogue of Viadana transformed into a carpentry shop, and the magnificent but crumbling synagogue of Sabbioneta deserted like its city.

I realized then that the history of the Jews in Italy was not only written in the large centers such as Rome or Venice, but also in the small villages and towns completely unknown to the Jewish people of Italy. I searched for other places throughout the country and found that the Jewish community has left its mark in all regions throughout its two thousand year history.

I began to write about these places in the Jewish magazine, Shalom. The decision to prepare this guide came when I realized that it would be too difficult to talk about all of these places in the limited space allotted in a monthly publication. I undertook this project not only with the intent of writing a history of the Jewish people of Italy, but rather with the intent of having people go out and visit these places and discover for themselves how widespread the Jewish roots are in Italy.

I am greatly indebted to Luca Fiorentino, who edited the chapters of Umbria, Abruzzo, Lazio, Puglia, Calabria, Sicily and Sardinia. An affectionate thank you is given to Paolo De Benedetti, who followed the various stages of research and compilation with patient care; to Laura Novatti, who has accompanied this book through all the technical and editorial phases; to Lia Levi and Luciano Tas, who put the City Room of Shalom Magazine at my disposal; to the librarians at the CDEC (Center for the Documentation of Contemporary Judaica) in Milan; to Vittore Colorni, Pier Cesare Ioly Zorattini, Emanuele Pacifici, Nello Pavoncello, and all of the other scholars, rabbis, and city officials who have enthusiastically accompanied me on my explorations.

Finally, a very special thanks to Tullia Zevi, president of the Union of Israelite Communities, who has given me many precious suggestions and incentives.

Annie Sacerdoti

Milan April, 1986

PREFACE

The first systematic survey of the oldest Jewish settlement outside of Israel coincides with an intense reawakening of interest in Italian Jewish history by various cultural, religious, and ethnic groups.

The Guide to Jewish Italy can be used as an instrument for research by the scholar, or as a compendium for the curious and motivated traveler. The Guide is a valuable resource for uncovering the past and the traditions expressed throughout the centuries by a community whose religion, culture, and presence have pervaded in inseparable unity to explain the Jewish case.

The Italian Jewish community is reputed by some as the oldest minority in the western world, and certainly the oldest collective in the Jewish Diaspora. It can boast a two-thousand year history and an uninterrupted presence on the Italian peninsula and islands. It is the last terminal of a tradition which, according to the historian Arnaldo Momigliano, "represents a component of Italian culture since the beginnings of Christianity, and even earlier."

During the Roman Empire, the Jewish population constituted 7 percent of the population. The Jewish community has continued to exist, in a minority status, in spite of a long history of humiliation and persecution inflicted by intolerance and prejudice.

The Jewish community has contributed to history by serving in a variety of roles. It was a meeting point between Ashkenazic and Sephardic Judaism, a place of dialogue between different philosophies and religions, and an economic bridge between north and south, and between east and west. Even in moments of greatest marginization, the community has never ceased to have a vital and symbiotic rapport with the rest of the population. It has positively created the thread of its own history.

The Jews were placed into a foreign society and continued to maintain their Jewish identity. They acted as a litmus paper and registered the degree of liberty and tolerance at various times. The pluralistic nature of Italian society has favored, perhaps more than anywhere else, the process of differentiated integration which made possible reciprocal enrichment between majority and minority.

Italy is scattered with tenuous and hidden traces, and impressions of the Jewish presence which are still significant and vital. It is said that there is not a corner of this country that does not have some trace. The historical, religious, and artistic patrimony of Italian Judaism is much more significant when you consider the almost total destruction of distinguished monuments and other testimonials of large Jewish groups in central and eastern Europe at the hands of the Nazis and their cohorts. Perhaps these people suffered from the same ills that afflicted the entire artistic-cultural patrimony of Italy, with the emigrations following the Racial Laws of the Fascists, and the mass deportations under the Nazi rule.

The youth have moved away from the old communities and settled in the large cities. Often, only a few elderly Jews are left behind. The results have been the decay of the old synagogues, thefts that often seem to have been commissioned, sales and selling-off of furnishings, community and private libraries, and of archives. Priceless ritual objects disappear, then reappear through mysterious channels in prestigious auctions, or in public or private collections in Italy and abroad.

The picture would not be complete without underlining the encouraging aspects. Communities such as Rome, Milan, Florence, Turin, Venice, Ferrara, and others rival each other in the promotion of artistic and cultural initiatives. Small and tiny communities manage to preserve the old heritage and the ancestral traditions, thanks to the consideration of a few willing people.

Numerous regional, provincial, and city administrations show a generous availability of restoration initiatives. The "Let's save what is salvageable" mentality is spreading. The cultural initiatives have multiplied. A reawakening of interest in our past is occurring everywhere. Even the younger generations are now searching for their roots.

The extermination of six million Jews and millions of other innocent victims cannot be forgotten or erased. Since the war, the first and second generation Jews have slowly learned to coexist with what can only be termed the "Holocaust Syndrome." Overcoming the confusion and desolation of the Post-War era, Italian Jewry has examined and rediscovered itself. There is a pressing desire to accept the struggle of its survival and to be reunited with its heritage. The reawakening of the collective memory allows Italian Jews to relive the past in the present with their eyes set on the future.

The memory of our ancestors has encouraged the Italian Jews to ask for and obtain from the Holy See, during the revision of the Concordato, the right to oversee and manage the ancient Jewish catacombs. The memory of communities which once flourished has induced us to institute in Rome, the Foundation for the Jewish Cultural Properties in Italy. The Bibliographic Center was created as well. These protective agencies were designed to document and salvage ancient ritual objects from the old Jewish communities.

The impulse to better understand ourselves and make ourselves understood is the basis for the work just finished by Annie Sacerdoti and Luca Fiorentino. I am greatly honored and moved by the invitation presented to me to write the Preface to this guide.

Tullia Zevi
Rome May, 1986

INTRODUCTION

The first Jews in Italy lived in Rome. They lived continuously in the "Eternal City" since the second century (B.C.E.), when Judah Maccabaeus formed an alliance with Rome. Starting as a small enclave, the Jewish community grew considerably after the destruction of the Temple in Jerusalem in the year 70. Thousands of Jewish slaves were deported to Rome and were used as workhands on the construction of the Colosseum.

The Jewish community in Rome was the largest in Italy. It was said to have a population of about ten thousand. They lived in groups between the Trastevere, Suburra, and Porto Capena. There were thirteen synagogues, each with its own internal autonomous charter, its own teachers, and leaders. The cemeteries and catacombs were located at Porta Portese, on the Appian Way, in Labicana and Nomentana.

The Jews left their mark on the city. Many Romans were impressed with the Jewish customs, the rigid monotheism, and the resting on the Sabbath. Some Romans actually converted to Judaism. Some Romans, on the other hand, derided the Jews and considered them barbaric because of their practice of circumcision.

Around the first century, the Jewish community in Rome was not the only one in the country. There were small enclaves in Venosa and Syracuse; Possuoli and Pompeii, in Campania; Taranto and Otranto, in Puglia; Ferrara, Brascia, and Milan, in northern Italy.

The Roman tolerance of the Jews diminished with the affirmation of Christianity and the Edict of Tessalonica of Teodosia (380), which recognized Catholicism as the official religion of the state. From that moment, tolerance was substituted with intransigence toward all non-Christian cults. Judaism, in respect to other religions, had one particular characteristic. Christianity was born from Judaism, and that historical and religious origin was respected. The Jews, however, had not recognized Jesus as the Messiah. They were therefore branded and discriminated against.

As the Empire declined in the following centuries, the papacy gained greater power. It would eventually control the lives of the Jewish people. From Gregory Magno (590-604), and for the next thirteen centuries, the history of the Roman Jewish community and those within the territories of the Catholic Church were subject to alternating swings, dependent on the attitude of each pontiff.

The Imperial rebirth of the Holy Roman Empire, under Charlemagne, changed the situation. Charlemagne nominated a special magistrate to defend the civil and commercial rights of the Jews. Under the Carolingian, some Jewish communities were established between Pavia and Verona. There was a relative period of tranquility during the 8th through 10th centuries. Under the Ottoman Empire, the Jews in southern Italy were able to develop great schools for Jewish studies. In Rome, Bari, Otranto, and in the numerous Sicilian communities, scholarly Jews were immediately recognized throughout Europe. The quotation from the prophet Isaiah (2:3), "For out of Zion shall go forth the law, etc." was paraphrased "From Bari shall go forth the law, and the word of the father from Otranto."

After the year 1000, the condition of the Jews throughout Italy was even more uncertain. It was subordinate and bound by the despotic will of feudal lords. Guilds of art and trade were being born during this period. Jews were barred from the guilds, since being Christian was a prerequisite to being a member of the guilds. The Jews were only permitted to participate in the business of moneylending and the sale of used clothing. Moneylending was forbidden by the Church for its own people, but permitted it for others. This fact is of incalculable importance. In an epoch in which the economy based on the barter system passed into a merchant economy, the control of investments and monetary circulation secured a primary commercial and financial role for those who held such control.

The loans served both the nobility and the common man. The noblemen required loans to finance their wars. The common people, whose living conditions were miserable, had to resort to small loans in order to survive. The noblemen granted the Jews the right to open pawn shops. They loaned money at a fixed interest rate, usually between 15 and 20 percent. The Jews were given the rights of residency only because of their moneylending activities. The pawn shops spread throughout all of Italy. They were located in the major urban centers as well as in the rural hamlets.

Along with the limitations of profession, there were other forms of discrimination. The Fourth Laterin Council of 1215, established that the Jews had to live in separate quarters. They had to wear recognizable insignia. Jewish men were required to wear a hat of a particular color and fashion (red and yellow) or a cloth badge on their coats. Jewish women were required to wear a yellow veil over their hats, similar to those worn by harlots. These provisions, however, were not carried out for more than a century, even in the Church states.

The conditions of the large Jewish community in Sicily were quite different. They lived in relative peace and tranquility under the Aragon (Spanish) rule, until the expulsion of 1492. Jewish doctors often frequented the Court where they were considered friends of the throne.

The Black Plague, which spread throughout Europe in 1348, gave way to new persecutions. Since the Jews remained untouched by the contagion, they were accused of spreading the disease by poisoning the wells. The Jews already lived in a separate section of the city. They followed particular and hygienic practices (for religious purposes) and the plague, therefore, did not find its way to their sections. The slander which was born and spread, especially in Germany, provoked massacres and subsequent flight. Many Jews found refuge in northern Italy, especially in the communities of Venice, Padua, Ferrara, and Mantua.

The first Age of Humanism and its spirit of openmindedness and conciliation favored the development of culture and letters. The "new science" of philology, love of language of the ancient sacred texts, included many works of Jewish origin. Immanuel ben Shlomo Romano (also known as the *Manoello Giudeo,* 1261-1328) wrote in the *volgare* (term for non-Latin, common Italian language) and in Hebrew. He wrote prose and poetry of the same genre as the *Vita Nuova* by Dante. His principal work *Machborot,* was well known in the Judeo-Spanish literature. His cousin, Yehudah ben Moshe (also known as *Guideo Romano,* 1291-1350), composed philosophical treatises.

In the next century, the situation improved considerably. In Ferrara, the Jewish community prospered because of the liberal practices levied by the Estensi family. In Florence, the Medici family protected those who loaned them money. The Piedmont region communities of Turin, Casale, Moncalvo, and Cuneo were enhanced with Jews from France. In the south and on the islands, however, the anti-Semitic attitude of Spain was being exacted.

New anti-Semitic ferment was occurring throughout Italy by the end of the 15th century. This was inaugurated by several minor priests. The most noted were Bernard of Siena, Giovanni of Capistrano, and Bernard of Feltre. It was in this climate that the episode of the child Simon took place. The Jews were accused of killing the child as part of a ritual murder. The trial, followed by death sentences, occurred in 1475. All of the Jews who lived in the Trentino region, and particularly those in Riva, were immediately expelled. The Jews placed an excommunication, or *chayrem,* on this region - no Jew was ever permitted to again live in this region.

A radical change in the history of Italian Jewry occurred in 1492. All Jews of Spain, and later Portugal, were expelled by King Ferdinand the Catholic. Many Jews took refuge in the Italian Jewish communities in Livorno, Ancona, and Venice. Within fifty years (1492-1541), Jews were also forced to leave southern Italy and the islands. It is estimated that over 37,000 Jews left Sicily during that period. Most of them moved to Rome, while others continued on to the Marche region (Ancona, Fano, Ascoli, and Camerino).

In the second half of the 16th century, the Church instituted the Counter-Revolution and assumed a rigid and intransigent attitude against the Jews. The anti-Semitic politics culminated with the Papal Bull (*cum nimis absurdum*), under which all Jews had to be enclosed in the ghettos. They could have no more than one synagogue, could not own property, and could only deal in used goods. At this point, Jews were required to wear the special identification markings (*contrassegno*). Many of these regulations, as had already been noted, were in existence prior to this dictate, but were only at this time found to have practical and regulatory applications.

The Roman Jews, immediately realizing the stringency of this Papal Bull, offered 40,000 scudi to have it abrogated. They did not succeed, and, in order not to be subjugated, fled from the papal state to others, where these ordinances and limitations did not exist.

The first ghetto was established in 1516, in Venice. Following this norm, came the creation of the ghetto in Rome (1555). In the following years, ghettos sprung forth in every city in Italy where there were Jews. Thus began the long and humiliating period of segregation which lasted until the Napoleonic Era.

The ghettos were very often unsanitary, narrow, with limited space, yet, no Jew ever went without a roof over his head. The spaces were subdivided and many unlikely areas were used. Corridors and stairways were transformed into rooms. New floors were built upon existing buildings. Some of these buildings reached eight and nine stories in height and were termed "skyscrapers."

The ghettos were poor quarters in which life unfolded with the learning of insecurity. They were always the first to be sacked during popular revolts and wars. Yet, the study of the Torah and the Talmud flourished. There were schools for the children and points of reference for Jewish merchants. The merchants traveled from city to city or to other countries and made the ghettos centers for the exchange of news and information. Paradoxically, in what should have been the most isolated part of the city, there were international rapports, thanks to the inexhaustive wandering of the Jewish people.

When the Jews were expelled from the Papal State in 1569 (excluding Rome and Ancona), many communities disappeared. Some of these were in the cities of Ravenna, Fano, Camerino, Orvieto, Spoleto, Viterbo, Terracina, and in the numerous communities of the Roman castles. Many families from the region of Lazio took refuge in the ghetto of Rome, but maintained a record of their origins in their surnames: Tagliacozzo, Di Veroli, Marino, Di Segni, and Di Nepi.

The anti-Semitic policy became a constant practice. Carlo Borromeo expelled the Jews from the Duchy of Milan in 1597. Venice threatened not to renew permission of residence to its old Jewish community. The only exception was Livorno, where the Grand Duke Ferdinand de 'Medici promulgated a liberal law showing great respect for the Jews. This attracted many merchants to the city who had been persecuted elsewhere. The Livornese Jews were also the only group never confined to a ghetto.

In the 1600s and 1700s, the conditions of segregation and instability did not disappear. The Jews were relegated to the margins of society and were looked down upon. They even found it difficult to practice moneylending. In the 15th century, the Christians were permitted to open pawn shops, *Monte di Pieta,* which proved to be strong competition against the Jewish businessmen. When

Napoleon arrived in Italy in 1796, he was greeted as a savior by the Jewish community. The doors of the ghettos were torn down and burned in the piazzas, under the "Tree of Liberty." For the first time in their history, the Jews felt like citizens with equal rights.

Only the Orthodox Jews openly disapproved of their brothers' enthusiasm for this exponent of a revolutionary and anti-religious French doctrine. They were not entirely wrong. The anti-Semitic prejudices accumulated over the centuries could not be removed suddenly. The very same revolutionaries suggested to Napoleon that the cost of the war be divided between the nobility,clergy, and the Jews.

In 1800, Jewish children were permitted to attend public schools, the sick were admitted to hospitals, and Jews were permitted to hold positions in public administration. In 1806, Napoleon created the *Sanhedrin* in Paris. This assembly was designed to reorganize the juridical life of all the Jewish communities in his Empire. One hundred and eleven notables arrived for this assembly. Thirteen members arrived from the Piedmont region and sixteen members arrived from the Italian Empire. No delegates from Tuscany or the Papal State came, since they were not under the jurisdiction of the French. The *Sanhedrin*, however, was not able to eliminate discontent or controversies, caused by severe restrictions imposed on the Jews in their trading practices.

Napoleon's defeat, and the "Restoration" signalled a pause in the Emancipation. The Jews were again thrown into the ghettos, and, in part, their equal rights taken away. Some restrictions which were more damaging to their personal dignity, such as the identification marking, were not reinstated.

1848 was the year of Emancipation for Piedmontese Jews. Carlo Alberto recognized the Jews as citizens and granted them full civil and political equality. The Jews were now politically active and joined secret societies, resurgent struggles, and wars of independence. After centuries of discrimination, the Jews now fought by the sides of other Italians against reactionary sovereigns and for the unification of the peninsula.

The Jews no longer had to camouflage themselves in public life. They no longer had to hide their places of worship. This was a time of constructing imposing and majestic synagogue buildings which became integral parts of the urban landscape. Great synagogues were built in Florence, Rome, Turin, Milan, Alessandria, and Vercelli. They were more similar in magnitude to Christian churches than the hidden synagogues (scoule) of the 1600s and 1700s.

The Emancipation changed the face of Italian Judaism in many other ways. Assimilation began, as did the abandoning of the old customs of their fathers, which had been conserved for centuries. In order to consider themselves true Italians, the Jews completely integrated themselves into the surrounding environment and often negated, whether consciously or not, their heritage.

In the beginning of the 20th century, Jews moved into the industrial centers and went into all trades including commerce, banking, the liberal professions, and public administration. Many Jews developed their small businesses into major industries. Some Jews joined the army, which had excluded Jews for centuries.

When the Fascists entered the government in 1922, the Jews were almost entirely integrated into the Italian society. They did not realize that the Fascists would later practice an anti-Semitic policy. Some Jews had taken part in the creation of the Fascist Party and had marched on Rome. Many Jewish businessmen and industrialists helped the Party financially, believing that they were defending their own economic interests and nationalistic ideals.

Some Jews held eminent public offices. Guido Jung was the Minister of Finance in 1932-33 and Ludovico Mortara was the president of the Appeals Court until 1923. Mussolini maintained an ambiguous attitude toward the Jews for a long time. He was suspicious of the relations with Jews of other countries and was afraid of the "International Jewish Conspiracy."

The agreement between the State of Italy and the Vatican was signed in 1929. Catholicism became the official religion of the state. The life of the Jewish communities was now regulated by the Falco Laws, which replaced by virtue of Article VIII of the Constitition, the principle of agreement between the state and the religious denominations other than Catholicism.

The discrimination and persecution of Jews began in 1930, when relations between Mussolini and Hitler strengthened. The anti-Semitism adopted spurious doctrines of racial persecution which was until then, unknown in the Italian tradition. In 1938, Mussolini published the "Manifest of Italian Racism," in which Fascism aligned itself with the Nazi ideology and declared the existence of a "Pure Italian Race."

In September of the same year, the declarations were followed by decrees and laws which expelled non-Italian Jews from the country. It banished Italian Jews from schools, army service, public service, and considered them second-class citizens. Some Jews converted to Christianity, thinking that it might save them. About five thousand left for Palestine, the United States, and South America. Some, like the editor Formiggine, chose suicide.

In 1940, Italy entered the war on Hitler's side. The Fascist squads were authorized to raid and sack Jewish communities. The synagogues in Trieste, Turin, Padua, and Ferrara were the first to be devastated. The Jews who remained in Italy were confined in camps. In 1943, the round-ups and deportations to the Nazi concentration camps began. It was total chaos. The Jews tried to find shelter in the Alps, in monasteries, or with courageous Christians who hid them in their homes. Some Jews joined the partisans. The youngest partisan was Franco Cesana. Other noted partisans include Eugenio Curiel and Rita Rosani.

When the war ended in 1945, the communities counted the survivors.

According to statistics compiled by Sergio della Pergola, 22,500 were missing from the roll-call. Approximately 7,500 were lost in the gas chambers and the massacres. Approximately 9,000 Jews emigrated and approximately 6,000 converted.

The Constitution of the Italian Republic reinstated all of the rights taken from the Jews under Fascism. The Jews were able to return to their studies, activities, professions, and were able to recuperate their possessions. Confusion and pain, however, was the general emotion. They did not realize the real and global dimensions of their enormous tragedy. They have just lost six million of their brethren.

Various events helped the communities in their recovery. The first was the birth of the State of Israel in 1948. When the United Nations Assembly confirmed the creation of the Jewish homeland in Palestine on December 2, 1947, the Jews united around the Arch of Titus in Rome to celebrate the event. For nineteen centuries, no Jew had ever passed under the monument, which was a symbol of Titus' triumph over the Jews of Palestine and of the destruction of the Holy Temple in Jerusalem in the year 70. During these celebrations of the birth of the State of Israel, the Jews of Rome danced joyously under the Arch.

After 1948, about 5,500 Jews, of which 3,500 were native born Italians, moved to the new State of Israel. They went to live in the land of their fathers. The majority of the Holocaust survivors, however, remained in Italy and began the reconstruction of their communities.

In the past forty years, Jewish life in Italy has prospered. Two communities alone, in Rome and Milan, make up the major part of the 40,000 Jews who live in the country. These same communities have been changing recently, with the influx of Libyan Jewish refugees in Rome and Iranian Jewish refugees in Milan.

Many communities have disappeared while many others are destined to follow. Records and the survival of the past remain and testify to the cultural patrimony of the Jewish people. Although the Jews have always been a minority, they have maintained their own identity for centuries and have resisted every attempt at annihilation.

This guide contains historical places which have survived as landmarks of the Jewish-Italian culture. We have highlighted the places in which Jewish life has existed, e.g. ghettos, roads, and synagogues. We have also documented the many cemeteries which recall the active presence of the old communities.

In doing this, an interesting phenomena has taken its course. A fervor of restorations, repairs, and documentation was started in the 1970s. This was assisted with contributions from the Assessors of Cultural Possessions. There has now been an reversal of tendencies, in respect to what occurred during World War II. The destruction and abandonment has been transformed into restoration. In the 1950s, several synagogue furnishings from extinct Jewish communities were sent to the new State of Israel and incorporated in new synagogues.

In the course of this volume, explanations of Jewish names, concepts, institutions, and holidays are not provided. For this purpose, we have added the glossary at the end of the text.

Medieval synagogue in Mantua.

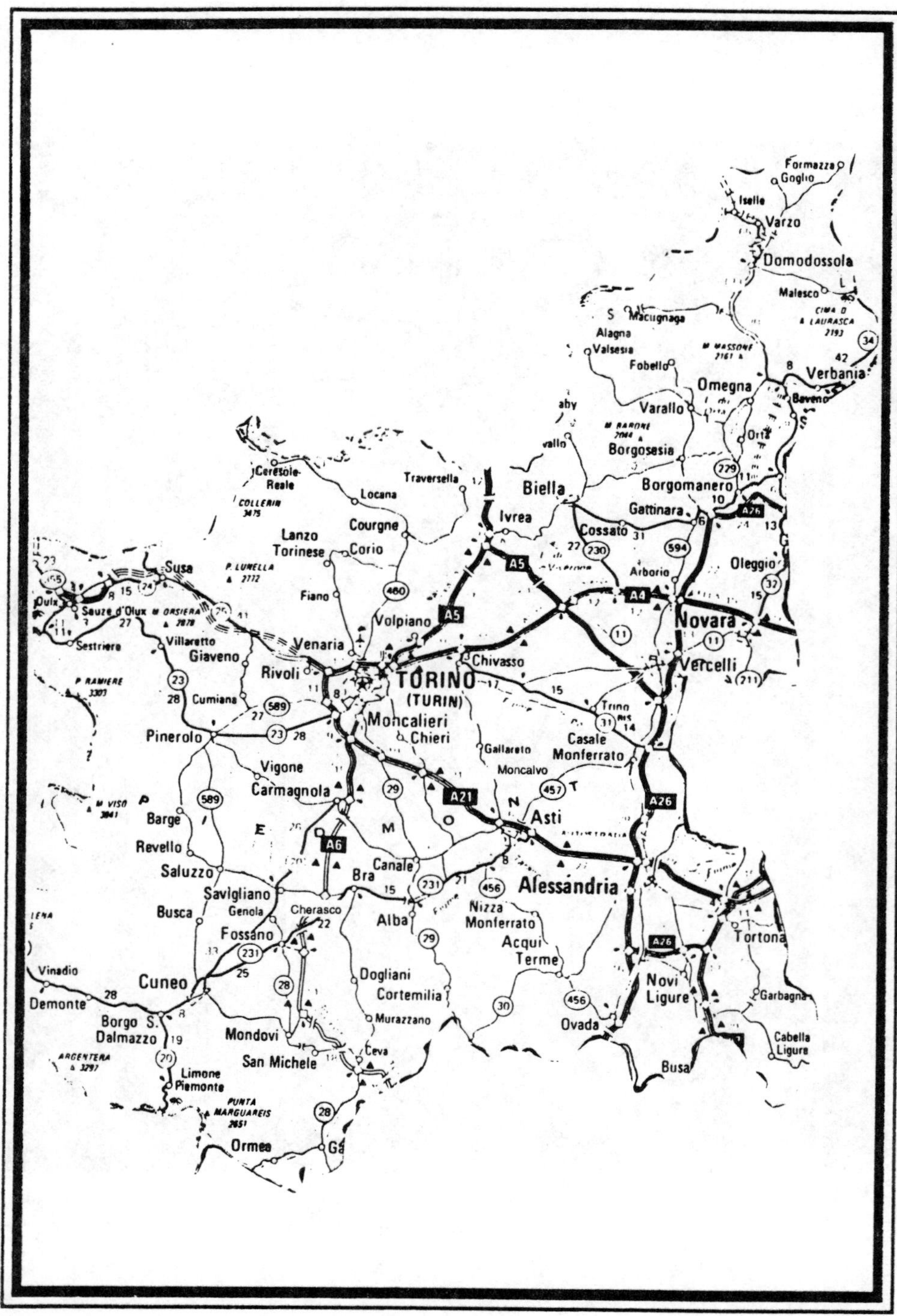
Formazza
Goglio
Iselle
Varzo
Domodossola
Malesco
Macugnaga
Alagna Valsesia
Fobello
Omegna
Verbania
Baveno
Varallo
Orta
Borgosesia
Borgomanero
Biella
Gattinara
Ivrea
Cossato
Arborio
Oleggio
Novara
Vercelli
Traversella
Ceresole Reale
Locana
Courgne
Corio
Lanzo Torinese
Susa
Oulx
Sauze d'Oulx
Sestriere
Fiano
Volpiano
Venaria
Villaretto
Giaveno
Rivoli
Chivasso
TORINO
(TURIN)
Moncalieri
Chieri
Cumiana
Pinerolo
Vigone
Carmagnola
Gallareto
Moncalvo
Trino
Casale Monferrato
Asti
Alessandria
Barge
Revello
Saluzzo
Savigliano
Genola
Busca
Cherasco
Bra
Canale
Alba
Nizza Monferrato
Acqui Terme
Tortona
Fossano
Cuneo
Vinadio
Demonte
Borgo S. Dalmazzo
Dogliani
Cortemilia
Murazzano
Mondovi
San Michele
Ceva
Novi Ligure
Garbagna
Ovada
Cabella Ligure
Busa
Limone Piemonte
Ormea
P. RAMIERE
M. VISO
ARGENTERA
PUNTA MARGUAREIS
A5
A4
A21
A6
A26

Piedmont Region

The first group of Jews arrived in the present day Region of Piedmont at the beginning of the 14th century. They had fled from France and Spain. The communal and individual exodus always made the Jews conspicuous. Extremely overcrowded communities were created during this exodus. In 1430, Amedeo VIII issued an edict which regulated the social and economic lives of the Jews. This *Sabaudiae Statute* was vigorously enforced until the Emancipation. The Jews were not permitted to construct new synagogues. They were not allowed to live near Christian homes. They were forced to wear identification markings, were not permitted to leave their houses during Holy Week, nor could they read Jewish books which were banned by the Church. The Christians were not permitted to harass or offend the Jews, nor force them into unwanted conversion. Over the course of centuries, however, these norms were applied with a certain elasticity and discretion, depending on the political climate and the financial needs of the rulers.

When the Edict was promulgated, there already existed important Jewish centers in Turin, Savigliano, Vercelli, Chieri, Cuneo, Mondovi, Nizza, and Asti. The communities of Casale Monferrato, which was under the rule of the Gonzaga family, and Saluzzo, which was under the rule of the Marquis of Saluzzo, were passed to the Savoys in 1630. All of these communities underwent periods of difficulty and uncertainty, followed by periods of tolerance and flourishment. Under Emanuel Filiberto (1553-80), a period of normal life appeared to open for the Jews. During his stay in Flanders, the sovereign was able to appreciate the commercial abilities and the interdependence of the Jews in these countries. When he returned to his Duchy, he favored the immigration and the establishment of Jewish merchants throughout his territories. In order to attract them, he planned to create a French port at Villafranca and at Nizza Marittima. His project was never realized as a result of opposition from the Vatican and their desire not to have competition in maritime trafficking.

Piedmontese Jews grew in number with the influx of expelled Jews from the neighboring Duchy of Milan (which was then under Spanish rule), Sicily, Sardinia, and the Kingdom of Naples. The Jewish condition worsened under the rule of Giovanna Battista di Nemours, the widow of King Carl Emanuel II. The sovereign, bowing to the pressures of France and the Papacy, imposed some of the anti-Jewish laws which were already in the Albertine Statute, namely the institution of the ghetto, which, until then, had only existed on paper.

In 1679, the first ghetto in the Piedmont region was created in Turin. Over the next few years, nineteen ghettos were created throughout the Duchy. These ghettos enclosed an estimated 5,000 Jews. The families who lived in isolated areas, or in towns which were too small to justify a ghetto, were forced to move to wherever there was a Jewish quarter.

These Jews were sometimes permitted to leave the ghettos in the evenings. The Jews of Cuneo could obtain this permission to attend the theater. These concessions, like that of not having to wear the markings or being able to live outside the ghetto in exchange for paying a tax, changed from one moment to another, and from one location to another. These changes were all subject to the will of the local authorities.

The Jews welcomed the arrival of the French with great enthusiasm. They were extended the rights proclaimed by the Revolution. The situation of the Jews, however, did not immediately change for the better. The doors of the ghettos were torn down, but the Jews remained. They waited for events to happen. They were not mistaken. A new wave of intolerance hit them when the Kingdom of Piedmont was occupied by Austro-Russian armies (1799-1800), which drove out the French. The Jews were again confined to the ghettos and were harassed by bands of religious fanatics.

Napoleon re-entered the Piedmont region after the victory of Marengo in 1800. The Jewish communities regained vitality. They were now equal to all citizens and entered, by right and de facto, into public office. Jews now held public office for the first time in the history of Italian Jewry. Neither the return to the throne of Victor Emanuel II, in 1814, nor the Restoration could annul these civil conquests. In 1816, he issued the *Regie Patenti,* which exempted Jews from wearing the identification markings. They could practice any trade unless it expressly required belonging to the Catholic Church. The Jews were permitted to leave the ghetto after sunset but had to return before 9 p.m. They had five years to sell the real estate they acquired under the French domination.

The true and definitive Emancipation came in 1848, When Carlo Alberto recognized the Jews as equal in rights with all of the subjects of the Savoy Kingdom. The Jews were euphoric. Communities designed grand synagogues to celebrate their Emancipation. They commissioned the greatest architects for these houses of worship. Many Jews moved away from the ghetto area, where they were forced to live for centuries, and settled in the large cities such as Turin. In the wake of this shift of Jewish populations, some old Jewish communities such as Chieri, Moretta, Carru, Savigliano, and Caragli disappeared. In some instances, new communities such as the one in Ivrea, were organized.

The strong Jewish presence in commerce and later in the textile industry is still recalled in a special jargon which was created by the people in the trades. Many Hebrew words have been incorporated in this jargon, which is used by both Jewish and non-Jewish workers. The expression, *Na vesta a kinim* (Dress of kinim), uses the Hebrew word *kinim.* Kinim is the Hebrew word for the third plague mentioned in the Bible. The ancient Egyptians were smitten with vermin or *kinim.* Italian literature has incorporated several Hebrew expressions. This occurred during the same period in which Yiddish expressions were being incorporated in central European literature.

The Falco Laws reorganized the Italian Jewish communities in 1930. It grouped the Piedmont region into only four communities: Turin, Casale-Monferrato, Alessandria, and Vercelli. The Racial Laws, the war, and the deportations hit the Piedmontese communities very hard. The Jewish population of nearly 4,000 was reduced to less than half at the end of the war.

There was an anti-Fascist intellectual environment in Turin. Carlo Levi wrote a diary of his internment in Turin "Christ Stopped in Eboli." Adriano Olivetti wrote about the function of a cultural laboratory of industrial literature which developed into the company which carries his name. Postwar Piedmontese writers of Jewish origin include such personalities as Natalie Ginzburg, Primo Levi, Sion Segre Amar, Guido Artom, and Augusto Segre.

ACQUI TERME

GHETTO SITE Via Portici Saracco #1

The first record of Jewish presence in this community dates back to the 16th century, but it is said that there were some Jews in the city as far back as the year 1000. The Jewish community disappeared before World War II.

JEWISH CEMETERY Via Romita #31

ALESSANDRIA

GHETTO SITE Via Milano and Via Migliara

There were Jews in Alessandria as early as 1490. Abramo, the son of Giuseppe Vitale de Sacerdoti, opened the first pawn shop in the city. Members of the Vitale family would later decide which Jewish families from France or Germany would be permitted to live in Alessandria. Alessandria was a major learning center. Its Rabbinical Academy brought forth many eminent scholars.

The ghetto was located in the vicinity of Via Milano. The interior passageways linked all of the houses of the ghetto with the synagogue. The Jews could move about freely without ever having to exit onto the street.

SYNAGOGUE Via Milano #5/7 Tel. (0131) 62224

The opening ceremonies of the synagogue in 1871, were attended by Rabbi Salomone Olper and Alessandro Foa, the Rabbi of Turin. The synagogue follows the Italian ritual. The ground floor contains a small "winter" chapel. The main sanctuary is located on the first floor. Its original Ark was destroyed by the Nazis. The present Ark was taken from the former synagogue in Nizza Monferrato. The second floor contains the Hebrew school and the offices of the Community.

JEWISH CEMETERY Viale Michel

The original cemetery was located near Porta Marengo, on the Piazza d'Armi. It was moved to the Viale Michel in 1820.

Interior of synagogue in Alessandria .

ASTI

SYNAGOGUE and MUSEUM Via Ottolenghi #8 Tel. (0141) *539-281*

The synagogue of Asti follows a special liturgy. It is known as *Appam,* which is derived from the Hebrew initials of the cities of Asti, Fossano, and Moncalvo. The liturgy is derived from a combination of the German and Old French rituals.

The synagogue was constructed in the early 1800s. It was reconstructed in 1889 by Jacob and Leonetto Ottolenghi. Its overall design remained substantially the same. The Bimah (reading platform) was moved from the center of the synagogue to the Ark wall. It is made from carved walnut and is encircled with a colored marble baluster. The windows were enlarged and replaced with stained-glass. The Ark dates from 1809. As the lavishly gilded Ark doors are opened, there is a small room which contains the Torahs. Above, is an elegant skylight. Some of the Torahs date back to the 1700s.

The front courtyard of the synagogue contains inscriptions which memorialize the people deported during the Second World War. The synagogue is used only for religious functions and occasional cultural activities, which are open to the public.

The museum is located on the first floor of the building. It contains liturgical manuscripts, Hebrew books which date back three centuries, silk vestments, and a brocade from the 18th century. This room was originally used as the "winter" synagogue. There is a permanent exhibit of the Resistance on the same floor. The Hebrew school was located at Via Aliberti #39.

GHETTO SITE Via Aliberti

The former ghetto was instituted in 1723 and was located along Via Aliberti, from the Sacco Pharmacy to the corner of Via Ottolenghi. There is a mural of the Madonna painted on the wall of the last house on Via Aliberti. This building once belonged to the Artom family. They were forced to paint this mural as a punishment for having windows which opened up to the outside of the ghetto.

JEWISH CEMETERY

The first cemetery was located between Via Antica Zecca and Via d'Azeglio. It was known as the "Meadow of the Jews." The present Jewish cemetery is located on Via Martiri Israelitici. Some of the notable figures buried in this cemetery include Rafael Beniam Artom, Isaac Artom, who was Secretary to

Pink marble columns surround Ark in the synagogue of Asti.

Cavour, and Zaccaria Ottolenghi, builder of the Alfieri Theater in Asti.

Note: The Bosca Company produces kosher wines in Canelli.

BIELLA

GHETTO SITE Corso del Piazza and Vicolo del Bellone

The ghetto in Biella was instituted in 1730. The Jonas, Vitales, and Olivettis were the prominent Jewish families in the city. There were less than sixty Jews in Biella on the eve of World War II. Biella was spared from losing any of its Jewish population to deportations.

SYNAGOGUE Corso del Piazza and Vicolo del Bellone #1

The small synagogue is located on the top floor of this building. The walls are decorated with lavish frescos. The synagogue is used only on special occasions. For further information, contact Mrs. Elvira Colombo at the Community Center of Vercelli at (0161) 66793.

JEWISH CEMETERY Via dei Tigli

The Jewish tombstones in this cemetery contain photographs of the deceased. This practice is rigorously prohibited by Jewish law. The tomb of Camillo Olivetti is located in this cemetery.

CARMAGNOLA

GHETTO SITE

The ghetto was created in 1724 and was located at Via Bellini, Via delle Cherche, Via Benso, and Via Baldassano.

ANCIENT SYNAGOGUE Via Bellini

The synagogue is located on the first floor of a 17th century house. The dimensions are 8.55 x 10.50 meters. All of the furnishings are 17th and 18th century Baroque and probably come from an older synagogue. This accounts for the apparent out-of-scale Ark and Tevah. The crown of the Tevah actually touches the low ceiling.

The polychromatic Tevah is located in the center of the room. The octagonal Tevah is painted gold, black, red, and dark green. It is capped with a large crown set upon eight columns. This Tevah, along with the Tevah of the former Chieri Synagogue (now located in the cellar of the Great Synagogue of Turin), are the most beautiful in the Piedmont region.

The Ark is located along the eastern wall of the synagogue. Its doors are richly engraved on their exterior and interior. The doors are flanked by two spiralled columns and stuccoed pilaster strips.

The last service in the synagogue was held for a wedding ceremony in 1939. It has been closed since that date. The synagogue is presently being restored by the Superintendent of Monuments of Piedmont and the Community of Turin. For further information about this synagogue, contact the Turin City Hall at (011) 685 585.

The Baroque Carmagnola Synagogue.

CASALE MONFERRATO

SYNAGOGUE and MUSEUM Vicolo Salomone Olper #44 Tel. (0142) 71807

The synagogue was built in 1595 and follows the German ritual. The exterior is nondescript and was designed this way as a security measure. The interior, however, is lavish. Visitors marvel at the splendor and richness of the synagogue. The Piedmontese Baroque triumphs in its precious furnishings and decorative murals.

The synagogue was built in 1595 as a rectangular space, with its major axis oriented in the north-south direction. Several families from San Salvatore took refuge in Monferrato in 1718 because the reigning sovereigns dissolved their synagogue. The synagogue was therefore enlarged due to the insufficient space. In 1868, the synagogue underwent radical transformations. The walls were dismantled and the space was enlarged. The ceiling was raised and an upper gallery for women was designed. The Tevah was taken from the center of the synagogue and placed in front of the Ark.

The community diminished in number over the years and the synagogue was in a state of disrepair. In 1969, the synagogue was completely restored to its original splendor. The work was supervised by architect Giulio Borbon, who is presently the acting director of the adjoining museum. The restoration was financed by the Superintendent of the Piedmont region. The synagogue was recently declared a national monument.

The work entailed restoring the brilliant original colors to the walls and to the decorations. A dark green square was left on the ceiling near the Ark to demonstrate how the synagogue looked before restoration.

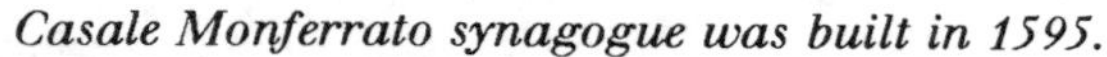

Casale Monferrato synagogue was built in 1595.

The synagogue measures 18 x 9 x 9 meters and is illuminated by fourteen windows. The walls are covered with inscriptions which record major events in the community's history, from its foundation to its Emancipation. There are two inscriptions that are noteworthy. The first inscription dates from 1629 and recalls the siege of the Spanish troops. The second inscription dates from 1656 and recalls when several bombs landed on the synagogue building but did not injure anyone. These two events were marked as special holidays, similar to the Holiday of Purim, which marked another period where the Jews were saved from annihilation. These holidays are known as the *Purim of the Spanish Siege* (21 Adar) and the *Purim of the Bombs* (7 Iyar).

There is an inscription on the wall which records the Emancipation, following the Albertine Statute of 1848. When Carlo Alberto died, the walls under the balconies were painted black, as a sign of mourning.

JEWISH CEMETERY

There are two Jewish cemeteries in Casale Monferrato. The oldest one is located on Via F. Negri #10. It is completely abandoned. The present cemetery is located on a private road, between Via Cardinal Massaia and Via F. Negri.

CHERASCO

GHETTO SITE Via Marconi and Via Emanuele

One of the clauses of the armistice between Napoleon and Vittorio Amadeo III of Savoy, provided that each family of the town offer a quilt to the French army. The ghetto inhabitants sent twenty-five.

ANCIENT SYNAGOGUE Via Marconi #4

Contact the Segre family at (011) 657 196 if you wish to visit the former synagogue building.

JEWISH CEMETERY Via Salita Vecchia

CHIERI

GHETTO SITE Via della Pace #8

Ark detail of Chieri Synagogue.

There has not been a Jewish community in Chieri since 1931. The Jewish quarter was located near the Church of San Domenico, between Via della Pace, Via Vittorio, and Vicolo Corona Grosso. There are records of a Jewish doctor being invited to live in the city in 1416, since there was no Christian doctor available. The first Jews arrived from France. They worked as moneylenders and in the wool and silk industries. Some were involved in the textiles trade while others were involved in gold and silver smithing.

The ancient synagogue is no longer extant. The Ark and Tevah were removed and placed into the cellar of the Great Synagogue of Turin in 1937.

JEWISH CEMETERY Vicolo San Stefano #1

Of the three cemeteries in Chieri, there is only one that is still utilized. Giacomo Segre participated in the liberation of Rome in 1870. His tombstone is found in this cemetery. His great grandson was a soldier in the Israel Defense Forces and was captured by the Syrian army during the Six Day War. He was publically executed before worldwide television cameras.

The other Jewish cemeteries are located on Via Nostra Signora della Scala #39 and on the Strada Statale #10. Contact Aldo Levi for further information at (011) 947 0337.

CUNEO

GHETTO SITE Via Mondovi #24

Cuneo was settled by Jews who were expelled in the 14th century from the Provence, the Papal States of southern France (Avignon). These "Juif du pape" were forced into the ghetto of Cuneo in 1724.

ANCIENT SYNAGOGUE Via Mondovi #18

The synagogue has been subjected to many transformations over the years. The last renovation was in 1884. The Ark is a splendid example of Venetian Baroque. There are large embossed Menorahs on the two gilded doors. There are depictions of the sacrificial instruments used by the priests in the Temple of Jerusalem. This iconographic motif is rare. Liturgical objects are commonly reproduced in the pages and frontpieces of medieval bibles, but rarely on sacred furniture.

To the left of the Ark towers the large elevated pulpit. This was installed during the last renovation and mimics the pulpits of the Catholic churches. On November 8, 1799, the City of Cuneo was under siege. The battles were raging between the French and Austro-Russian troops. During a religious service, a bomb landed in the synagogue. That bomb never exploded and is still lodged in

Synagogue of Cuneo.

the synagogue wall, under the rabbi's pulpit! The Jewish community celebrates the *Purim of the Bomb*, in memory of that miraculous event.

The former Hebrew school was located on the first floor of the building. Although the school has not been used for many years, the original furnishings, benches and even an abacus, have been left intact.

If you wish to visit the ancient synagogue, contact the Cavaglion family at (0171) 60891 or 2007.

During the siege of the city, Abramo Lattes was able to get a message through the enemy lines and thereby saved the city. In honor of this courageous act, the city fathers changed the weekly Saturday open market in the Piazza Galimberti to Friday, so that the Jewish community could participate.

JEWISH CEMETERY Via Bassa San Sebastiano

The old Jewish cemetery was expropriated for the construction of a highway in 1936. The Jews were given a section of the community cemetery that same year. There is one tombstone which records a tragic event, the death of five Jews who were killed on the last day of World War II.

FOSSANO

JEWISH CEMETERY Via Orfanotrofio #17

IVREA

GHETTO SITE Via Quattro Martiri

The first Jews settled in this city in 1547. The Olivetti family arrived in the following century. The Jews were forced to live outside the castle walls, on Via Palma (today's Via Quattro Martiri), following the plague of the mid-1600s.

In 1801, the ghetto was under siege by a band of brigands. The Jews defended their small community by using an ingenius strategy. They took twenty-five horsemen and had their horses pound noisily. They then sounded their trumpets. The bandits thought that there was an entire platoon of soldiers within the ghetto walls, and quickly ended their siege.

The growing industrial development in the 19th century brought many Jews to Ivrea. They were employed in the Camillo Olivetti Company.

SYNAGOGUE Via Quatro Martiri #20

The synagogue was built in 1870. It has recently been restored by the Piedmont Superintendents of Monuments. The adjoining social hall is also being restored. There has been a recent resurgence of Jewish life in Ivrea due to the Olivetti Company. Jewish employees have taken up residence in the city.

JEWISH CEMETERY Via Mulini #30

There are several graves of Jewish Polish and Russian soldiers in this cemetery. The former Jewish cemetery was located at Porta Aosta. There is no trace of that cemetery.

MONCALVO

GHETTO SITE Via General Montanari and Via IV Marzo

ANCIENT SYNAGOGUE Piazza Castello #29

The synagogue furnishings were sent to Israel.

JEWISH CEMETERY

The ancient cemetery is still in use. For further information, contact the Norzi family at (0141) 917 931.

Note: The Borganino Agricultural Company produces kosher wines.

19th century Ark from Moncalvo, now at Ponevez Yeshiva, Israel.

MONDOVI

GHETTO SITE Via Vico

The Jews in the upper part of the city (Mondovi Piazza) practiced moneylending. The Jews living in the countryside raised silkworms and produced silk. The ghetto was established in 1730 and was located in the area of Via Vico, from Vicolo Pizzo to the Piazza d'Armi.

ANCIENT SYNAGOGUE Via Vico #65

The synagogue of Mondovi is a gem. The octagonal Tevah is made from sculpted wood and is partially gilded. It is located in the center of the synagogue. The golden Ark is located along the eastern wall and dates from the 1700s. Five large crystal chandeliers illuminate the synagogue. The right wall is frescoed with an illusionary perspective. There are fourteen false windows, adorned with elegant blue drapes, painted on this wall. Biblical verses are written on the architraves. The entire upper part of the synagogue is frescoed with ornamental motifs.

This small synagogue was partially restored by the Jewish Youth Organization, with the assistance of expert craftsmen. If you wish to visit this ancient synagogue, contact Marco Levi at (0174) 42555.

JEWISH CEMETERY Viale Cimitero

The old 16th century cemetery was found under the ramparts of the citadel. It was in the area where thousands of people, who died during the plague of 1630, were buried. It is recognizable at the first large curve on the bulwark, Emanuele Filiberto. This old cemetery was closed in the early 1800s. The present cemetery is located on the Viale Cimitero. On the access road, there is a stone tablet which honors the victims of the Holocaust.

NIZZA MONFERRATO

GHETTO SITE

The first Jews arrived in 1539 but were not required to live in a ghetto until 1732. The ghetto was located in a few houses on Via Massimo d'Azeglio, near the Piazza Martiri di Alessandria. The synagogue was located in the grand Palazzo Debenedetti. Its furnishings were sent to the synagogue in Alessandria.

REMEMBRANCE PARK Via Ponte Verde #5

Part of the community cemetery has been declared a "Remembrance Park," and memorializes those Jews who died during World War I.

Tomb of De Benedetti.

SALUZZO

GHETTO SITE Via Deportati ebrei

Jews lived in the countryside for over two centuries before they were confined in the ghetto in 1724. Ghetto life was relatively tranquil. The Jews were moneylenders, jewelers, cobblers and were involved in selling second-hand clothing.

ANCIENT SYNAGOGUE

The first synagogue was built inside an existing building within the ghetto walls in the early 1700s. It was rebuilt in 1832. The seating capacity was 300. The synagogue has been closed since 1964. If you wish to visit the ancient synagogue, call Vittorio Segre at (0175) 43026.

JEWISH CEMETERY Via di Pagno and Via Lagnasco #5

SAVIGLIANO

GHETTO SITE Via Alfieri

TRINO

GHETTO SITE Corso Italia #47

The ancient synagogue was built in the 16th century. It was housed in this building. Its furnishings were shipped to a new synagogue in Ramat Gan, Israel, in 1965.

JEWISH CEMETERY Via C. Battisti

TURIN (Torino)

GHETTO SITE

The ghetto was instituted by the Savoys in 1679. The former Mendicanti Hospital served as the ghetto. It housed 763 Jews. There were 527 very small rooms. Additional space was created by converting storage rooms into living quarters. The building was located at the junction of four roads; Via Maria Vittorio, Via Bogina, Via Principle Amedeo, and Via San Francesco de Paola.

In less than fifty years, from 1737 to 1794, the Jewish population grew to approximately 1,300. As a result, the "new ghetto" was instituted in the area bound by Via Francesca, Via des Ambois, and the Piazza Carlina. Approximately 300 people lived in this area. Four families (the Todros, Levis, Ghidiglias, and the Malvanos) paid a hefty sum to the sovereigns and were thereby permitted to live outside the ghetto.

The ghetto was opened for the first time by Napoleon's troops. It was completely dismantled in 1848, when King Carlo Alberto instituted the "Albertine Statute." The gates of the ghetto are still recognizable at Via Maria Vittorio #325 and at Via des Ambois #2. These are the original four and five story structures of the ghetto. Some buildings which had façades facing outside of the ghetto were required to seal-up all of their windows. The Jews were only permitted to have windows which faced the interior courtyards of the ghetto. One of the three synagogues in the ghetto was located in the courtyard at Via Bogina #17.

MOLE ANTONELLIANA Via Montebello and Via Giuseppe Verdi

In 1861, the Jewish community commissioned architect Alessandro Antonelli to design its new synagogue. This building was to become the symbol of Jewish emancipation. Its majesty was designed to cancel the long centuries during which the Jews suffered discrimination and persecution. The steel frames of the structure were erected and exterior walls were constructed. However, after more than ten years of construction and cost overruns, the Jewish community was forced to sell the unfinished structure to the City of Turin. It was ultimately completed and designated as the Museum of National Independence. This structure is now a national monument and is known as the Mole Antonelliana, or the Tower of Antonelli. It is equal in size and grandeur to the Eifel Tower in Paris.

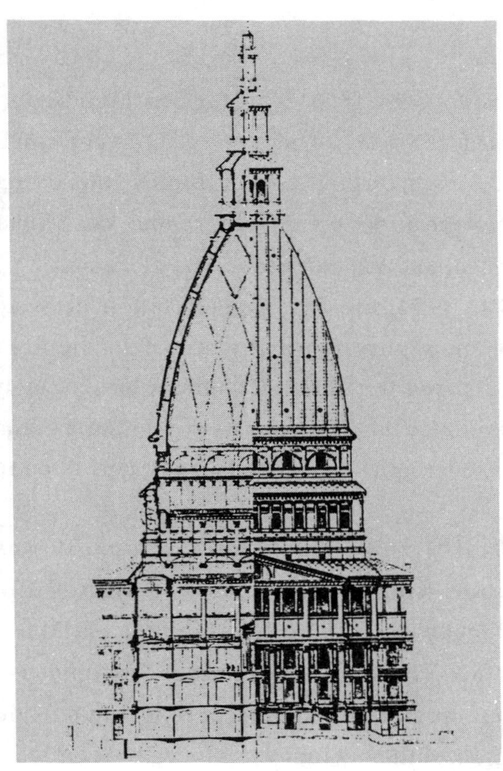

Mole Antonelliana,
Section and elevation.

Turin's Mole Antonelliana was originally built as a synagogue.

GREAT SYNAGOGUE Via Pio V #12 Tel. (011) 658 585

The Great Synagogue of Turin was inaugurated on February 16, 1884. It was designed by Enrico Petiti and took four years to build. The Moorish Revival structure is capped by four onion-domed towers. The main sanctuary measures 35 x 22 x 16 meters and seats 1,400 people. The women's galleries are supported by massive granite columns. The original structure was highly ornamented. The ceilings were designed with coffers.

On November 20, 1942, a small bomb landed on the synagogue during an aerial attack. The damage was devastating. Wooden structures, plaster, and furnishings were completely destroyed. At the end of the war, only the towers and the perimeter walls remained. In September, 1945, the Civil Engineers of Turin, in an attempt to save the edifice, began a series of reinforcements. The synagogue remained unfurnished and without covering until 1949. At that time, the interior decorations were restored with marble and stucco, along the colonnade and the Ark wall. The Ark is located along the eastern wall. The seating plan is typical of post-Emancipation synagogues and is similar to the seating plan of a Christian church. The main sanctuary is used only on major Jewish holidays.

There is a small museum in the wing adjoining the women's gallery. This was prepared for the Centennial celebration of the synagogue and has become a permanent exhibition. There are ritual objects made of finely engraved silver and embroidered clothes which date back to the 18th and 19th centuries.

There are two small chapels in the cellar of the synagogue. These are used as daily chapels. They were constructed in 1972 in the underground vaults which, until then, had been used as storage areas. Architects Giorgio Ottolenghi and Giuseppe Rosenthal designed these chapels.

The first "Tempietto" is designed in the form of an amphitheater. The Ark and Tevah (reading platform) are Baroque in style, and have been brought from the former synagogue in Chieri. This chapel follows the Italian ritual. The Tevah is positioned in the center of the room, as was common in synagogues predating the Emancipation. The perimeter walls are red brick.

The second "Tempietto" is located in an adjoining room. It is smaller and more secluded. It is used for daily functions. Its Ark was built in the 1700s and was used by the German Jews who lived in an area once known as the "new ghetto." It was moved to a rest home in Piazza San Giulia, where it remained until 1963.

Turin's Great Synagogue.

The old Chieri synagogue furnishings are housed in Turin's Great Synagogue.

In 1849, the Ark was painted black as a symbol of mourning for the death of Carlo Alberto, the king who had given the Jews their Emancipation. The Ark is still painted in that dark hue.

The Emanuele Artom Library is located in the same area in the cellar. It contains 4,000 volumes in Italian and 6,000 volumes in Hebrew. The library was organized in the City of Vercelli. The Benvenuto and Alessandro Terracini Archives of Jewish Customs and Traditions was created with a gift from the Terracini brothers, who originate from Asti. They donated 4,000 volumes from their personal library. Many of these volumes date back to the 1500s. Among the special items in the collection are several volumes which have annotations in the margins, written in Portuguese. This is proof of the Iberian origin of some of the Jews in the Piedmont region.

The Community Center adjoins the Great Synagogue. It houses the community offices, the rabbi's office, and the Margulies Disegni Rabbinical Academy. The Hebrew school and the Jewish Rest Home are located around the corner, at Via San Anselmo #7. The complex also houses the ADEI-WIZO, the Piedmontese Zionist group, the Keren Hayesod Commission, the Group of Hebraic Studies, and the Hashomer Hatza'ir.

If you wish to eat a kosher meal, call the Community Office at (011) 658 585.

JEWISH CEMETERY

The first Jewish cemetery of Turin was in the Escarpe du Bastion de San Jean de Dieu. The documents describing its location were written in French. It was located between Via Maria Vittorio and Via delle Rosine. It was closed in 1772 and replaced by the cemetery at Vanchiglia (hors de la porte du Po, a main gauche du Faubourg). It was in use until 1867. In that year, a Jewish section of the community cemetery was established on Corso Regio parco.

Tombstones of the older cemetery were transferred to this new section. The oldest tombstones are made of granite and date back to 1500-1600. At that time, only the names of the deceased were inscribed. Jewish dates were not inscribed. The oldest tombstone that has been deciphered is that of Hanna Falco. All of the other ancient tombstones have corroded from exposure to weather and humidity. The names are no longer legible.

VERCELLI

GHETTO SITE Via Elia Emanuele Foa

The first Jews arrived in Vercelli in the 1400s. They later welcomed Jewish refugees fleeing from the Inquisitions of Spain, Portugal, and southern Italy. The first ghetto was instituted in 1727. Its gates were located at the mouth of Via Foa and Via Gioberti; at the narrowest point of Via Foa, before the churchyard of the Church of San Giuliano; in the middle of Via Castelnuouvo delle Lanze; and in the narrowest part of Via Morosone. The Jewish community was required to pay for the installation of these gates.

SYNAGOGUE Via Foa #56

In 1864, the community invited the noted Jewish architect, Marco Treves, to design their synagogue. He was involved in the design of the Great Synagogue of Florence. He was also the Superintendent of the Louvre Museum in Paris. The designs he submitted were too grandiose and were too costly for the congregation. Ten years later, the congregation called upon the engineer, Giuseppe Locarni, for a second design. The plans were approved and, in 1878, the synagogue was completed. In honor of the opening of the synagogue, the congregation minted a bronze medallion to commemorate the event. On the front was a perspective view of the synagogue. On the back was the date of the inauguration.

The synagogue followed the German ritual. It was designed in the Moorish Revival style. The congregation has diminished in size and the synagogue is now in a state of ruin. The interior walls are chipped; the structural framework is in danger of collapse, and the many stained-glass windows have been smashed by vandals. The Torahs and some of the furnishings have been removed and stored in the Great Synagogue of Turin. If you wish to visit this synagogue building, contact Mrs. Elvira Colombo at (0161) 66793. The Community Center of Vercelli is located at Via Foa #70.

JEWISH CEMETERY Corso Randaccio #24

This is the fifth cemetery since the 1400s. The first Jewish cemetery was on a plot near the Church of San Giacomo. The site is presently the location of the military recruiting office. The second cemetery is still extant and is located on Via Manzoni, near the Visitazione Monastery. The next cemetery was located at the corner of Via Melchiorre Amadeo Bodo and Via Rodolfo Gattinara di Zubiena. The last Jewish cemetery was located at Via Conte Verde, near the railway circle.

MEMORIAL PLAQUE Corso Italia #44

The stone tablet memorializes Giuseppe Leblis, the former president of the Jewish community, who was deported to Auschwitz in 1943.

The synagogue in Vercelli now stands abandoned.

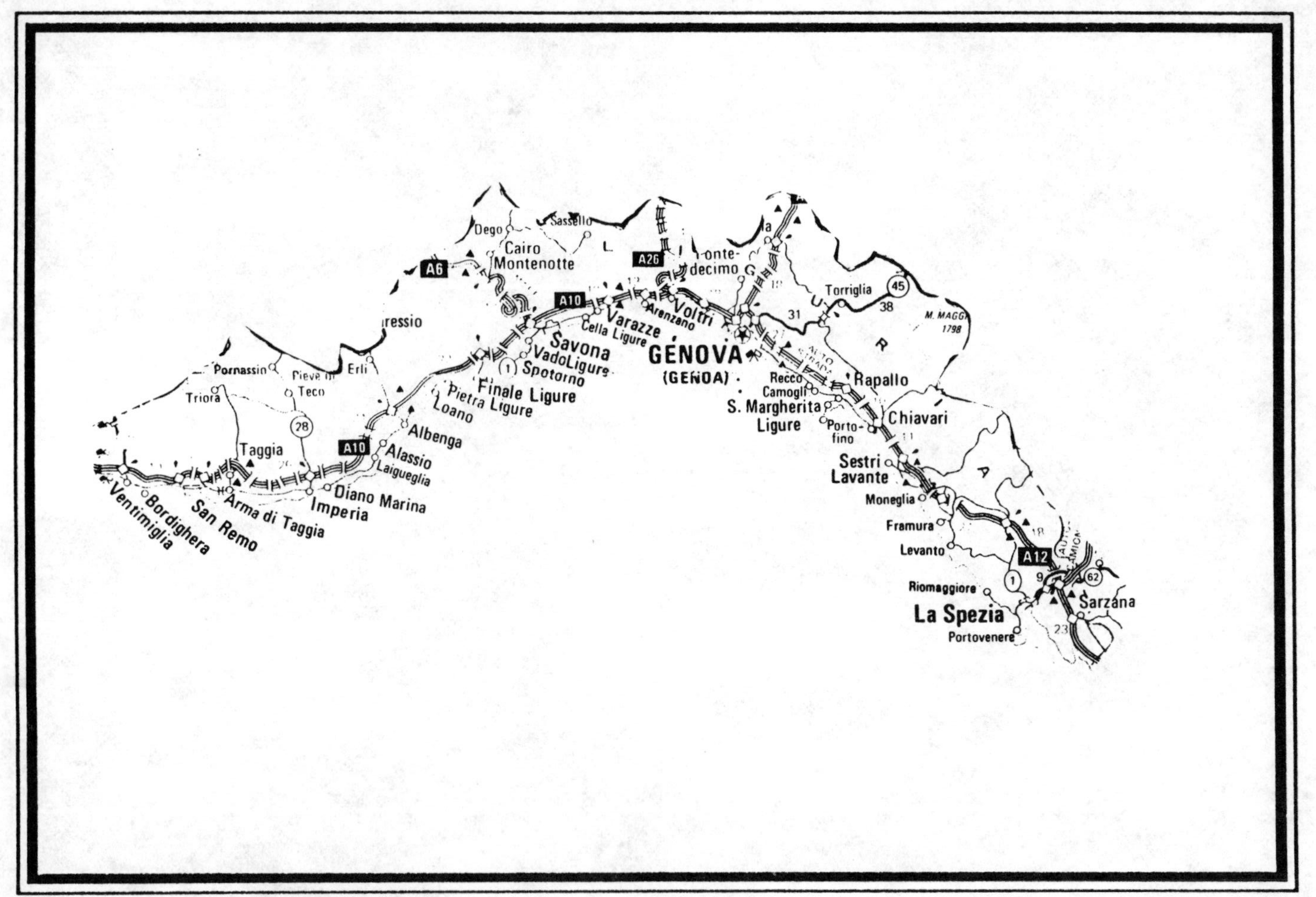
Dego
Sassello
Cairo
Montenotte
A6
A26
Pontedecimo
A10
Torriglia
45
38
M. MAGG
1798
Savona
Vado Ligure
Spotorno
Varazze
Cella Ligure
Arenzano
Voltri
GENOVA
(GENOA)
Pornassio
Pieve di
Teco
Erli
Triora
28
Finale Ligure
Pietra Ligure
Loano
Albenga
Recco
Camogli
S. Margherita
Ligure
Portofino
Rapallo
Chiavari
Taggia
A10
Alassio
Laigueglia
Diano Marina
Imperia
Arma di Taggia
San Remo
Bordighera
Ventimiglia
Sestri
Lavante
Moneglia
Framura
Levanto
A12
62
Riomaggiore
La Spezia
Portovenere
Sarzana

Liguria Region

There have been small Jewish settlements throughout the Liguria region as early as the 6th century. Savona hosted a group of Jewish bankers in 1450 but later expelled them when the *Monte di Pieta* was opened. The Jews lived in the *Vicolo dei Giudei* (Jews Street), now called the Vico Crema. In 1452, the Jews in Savona were accused of ritual murder. There were additional accusations in the cities of Megli (near Recco) and Novi (near Alessandria). These accusations occurred under the Papacy of the Ligurian Pope Sistine IV (1471-1484).

There have been Jewish settlements in the cities of Gavi, Sarzana, Chiavari, and Lerici. The only remains of a ghetto are found in Lerici. It was located on Via del Ghetto and Via Revellino. The hinges of the ghetto gates are still found at the entrance, along Via del Ghetto.

Two varieties of palm trees are cultivated in the City of Bordeghera. One variety, called *Romano,* is used by Catholics on Palm Sunday. The other variety, called *Ebraica,* is used by Jews during the holiday of Succot. Each palm tree has a different color. This is achieved by tying the branches together. The *Romano* palm is tied in September and untied two weeks before Palm Sunday. Its color is pale yellow. The *Ebraica* palm is tied in July and unbound in September, just before the holiday. Its color is green.

During the Catholic Holy Week, a Passion Play, *Turba gei giudei* (Mob of Jews), is presented in the cities of Castellaro, Pantasina, Riva, Bussana, Vallebona, and Taggia.

ALASSIO

Synagogue services are conducted during the summer only at the Villa Gouyot, on the Viale delle Palme #7, on the corner of Corso Europa.

GENOA (Genova)

The few Jews who came to Genoa in the 6th century were not permitted to stay longer than three days. When Benjamin of Tudela, the Jewish Marco Polo, visited the city in 1159, he noted in his diary that there were only two Jewish families of Moroccan descent, who ran a dye-works.

A large group of Jews arrived in 1492, following the expulsion from Spain. They were not greeted receptively by the city. Many Jews were told to continue traveling to Livorno, a more hospitable port. Genoa maintained a cautious attitude toward the Jews. Some say that it was Church policy. Others claim that the Jews posed a threat to the commerce and industry. The first great plague hit Genoa in 1492. It was said that the Jews had brought the disease.

The first official Jewish community was established in 1658, when Genoa became a French port. The authorities permitted Jews to participate in trading and business.

GHETTO SITE Vico del Campo

The ghetto was established in 1660. It was located on the Vico del Campo and consisted of a small plaza and a dark alleyway. It was once known as "Jews Alley." The second ghetto was established in 1674 and was located near the Piazza dei Tessitori (Plaza of the Weavers), near the Church of Agostino.

In 1675, many Jews left the city since they refused to comply with all of the rigid requirements such as wearing identification markings, paying high taxes, listening to compulsory sermons in the churches, and being confined in a ghetto. The ghetto was soon dismantled.

The few Jews who remained in the city organized the first synagogue, which followed the Sephardic ritual. It was located near the Malapaga Wall.

SYNAGOGUE Via Bertora #6 Tel. (010) 891 513

In 1935, the Jewish community of Genoa numbered 2,500. It built a new synagogue which was designed by architect Francesco Morandi. The

Synagogue of Genoa.

furnishings from the old synagogue were transferred to this building. The old building was destroyed during bombings in World War II.

The Moorish Revival structure is a massive square, covered with ashlars of stone, and is crowned with a dome. The ground floor contains the small "winter" chapel and utilizes the furnishings from the 18th century Malapaga (ghetto) synagogue. The main sanctuary is designed as an amphitheater. The furnishings are modern. The walls of the Ark area are covered with green marble from Polcevera. There are two levels of women's balconies. The stained-glass windows were designed by Emanuele Luzzati in 1959. The adjoining Community Center houses the rabbi's office, mikveh, and Hebrew school, which closed in the 1950s.

Fascism hit the community very hard. In November, 1943, three hundred Genovese Jews were arrested and deported. Among them was the brave Rabbi Riccardo Pacifici, who would not leave his community, as it was deported. A small memorial stone in front of the synagogue is dedicated to his memory.

The *Delasem*, a relief agency for Jewish refugees, helped over 30,000 Jews from 1936 until after the war. Many Jews were smuggled into Palestine before the State of Israel was created. They left from the Port of Genoa.

In 1969, the Jewish community of Genoa named a street in honor of Theodor Herzl. At the same time, a street in Haifa was named after Giuseppe Mazzini. There are today, approximately 650 Jews living in Genoa.

JEWISH CEMETERY

The first Jewish cemetery was located behind the old wall of the city. It was established in the 1700s. In the beginning of the 19th century, the Jews were assigned a new location. It was called the "cave," and was located near the sea, at the end of Via Corsica, near the Lungomare Aurelio Saffi.The present Jewish cemetery is located at Staglieno. It was established in 1886.

Jewish cemetery, Genoa.

SAN REMO

JEWISH CEMETERY

Many foreigners came to San Remo for cures during the 1880s. Those who were not cured were buried in this Jewish cemetery.

LA SPEZIA

SYNAGOGUE Via XX Settembre #165 Tel. (0187) 33131

In 1965, the City of La Spezia named a school in memory of Adriana Revere, a nine-year-old Jewish girl who was deported by the Nazis.

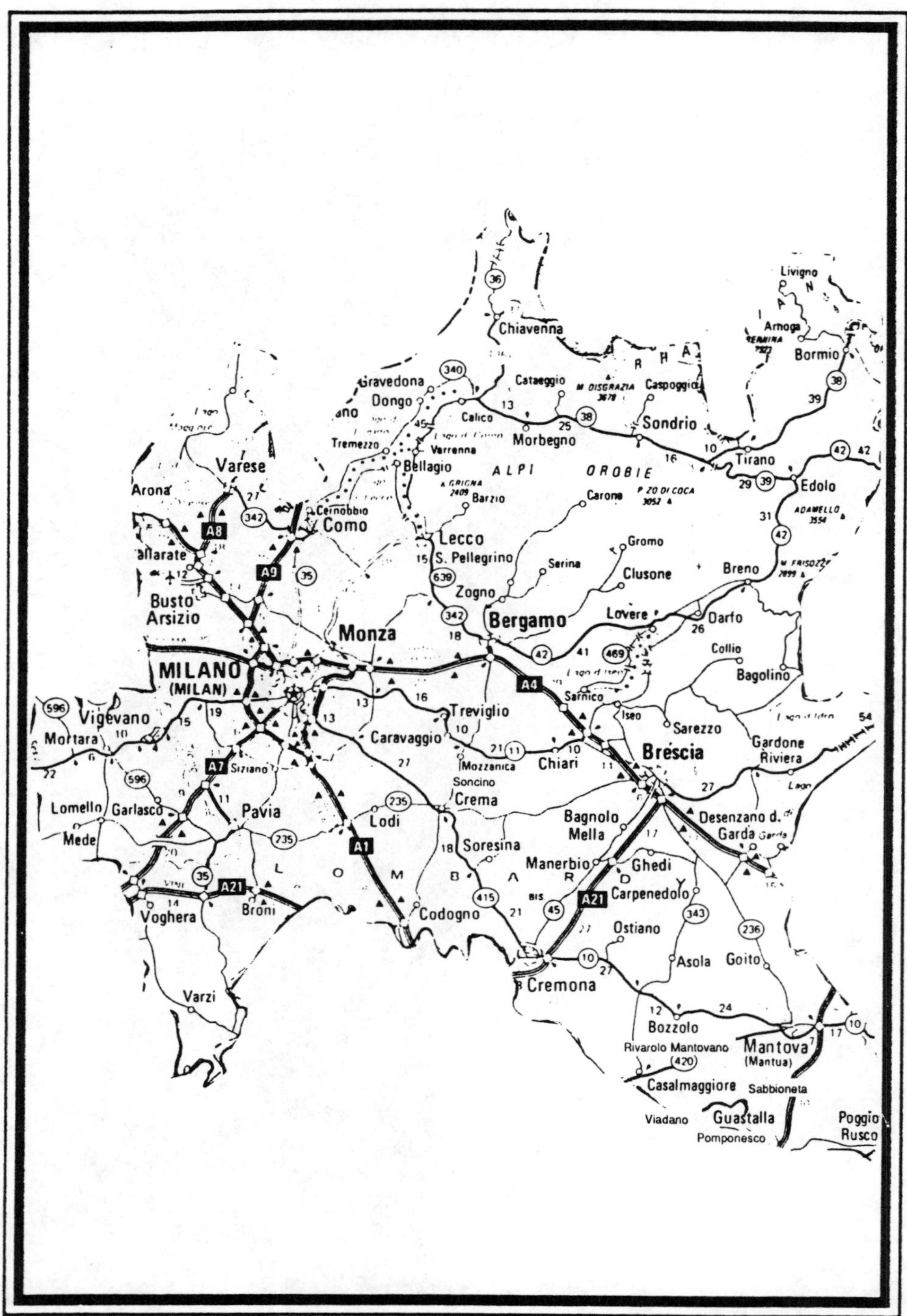

Livigno
Bormio
Chiavenna
Gravedona
Dongo
Tremezzo
Varrenna
Bellagio
Calico
Cataeggio
Caspoggio
Morbegno
Sondrio
Tirano
Edolo
ALPI
OROBIE
Barzio
Carona
Varese
Arona
Cernobbio
Como
Lecco
S. Pellegrino
Zogno
Gromo
Serina
Clusone
Breno
Busto Arsizio
Monza
Bergamo
Lovere
Darfo
Collio
Bagolino
MILANO
(MILAN)
Vigevano
Mortara
Treviglio
Sarnico
Iseo
Sarezzo
Caravaggio
Chiari
Brescia
Gardone Riviera
Siziano
Mozzanica
Soncino
Crema
Lomello
Garlasco
Pavia
Lodi
Mede
Bagnolo Mella
Desenzano d. Garda
Soresina
Manerbio
Ghedi
Carpenedolo
Voghera
Broni
Codogno
Ostiano
Asola
Goito
Cremona
Varzi
Bozzolo
Rivarolo Mantovano
Mantova
(Mantua)
Casalmaggiore
Sabbioneta
Viadano
Guastalla
Pomponesco
Poggio Rusco
A1
A4
A7
A8
A9
A21

Lombardy Region

DUCHY of MILAN

There is evidence of a Jewish presence in this region as early as the Holy Roman Empire. The community in Pavia was small in 1387. It had a synagogue and a cemetery. In 1597, the Jews were expelled. Nothing of that community has survived.

Francesca Sforza granted many liberties to the Jews living in Cremona in 1442. They were not required to wear the special identification markings. Cremona was the most important Jewish center in the 16th century. There was a great Rabbinical Academy and a major publishing center for Jewish books. Vicenzo Conti printed 10,000 volumes of the Talmud and sold 20,000 Jewish manuscripts in 1559. Today, there are very few traces of that Jewish community.

In the 15th century, Israel Nathan left Germany and arrived in the City of Soncino. He created the famous publishing house. He adopted the name of the city and was later known as Israel Nathan Soncino. In 1488, he was accused, along with 37 other Jews, of publishing books which contained offensive ideologies against the Catholic Church. The list of the accused shows that many came from towns, which until recently, were believed to have no Jewish presence: Broni, San Colombano, Monza, Novara, Vigevano, Mortara, Lodi, Bregnano in Radadda, Vailate in Radadda, Rivolta in Radadda, Bocca d'Adda, Casalmaggiore, San Giovanni in Croce, Catelnovetto, Valenza, Mandello, Como, Castellazzo, Castelnuouvo Scrivia, Voghera, Castelleone Cremonese, Vighizzolo, and Arena Po. The trials ended with the deaths of nine Jews. The others were required to pay a fine of 19,000 ducati.

The life of the Jewish community in the Duchy of Milan was characterized by alternating expulsions, extensions, and condemnations. The minor priests, Bernard of Feltre and Michele Carcano, incited the people against the Jews. The Jews were accused of ritual murder in Arena Po. While the trial was in progress, the "missing" child reappeared. Nevertheless, the Jews were expelled from the Duchy of Milan in 1597.

The Jews took refuge in the nearby cities of Mantua, Modena, Reggio, Fiorenzuola, Monferrato, and Venice. Jews were permitted to live in the City of Milan (versus the Duchy of Milan) for three-day intervals. They had to stay in the "red light" district of the city, known as Buttonuto. In 1580, the Spanish governor of Milan granted the Jews a twenty-day stopover. The Jews returned to the Duchy and the City of Milan in 1714, when Lombardy fell to the Austrians.

DUCHY of MANTUA

The history of the Jews of Mantua has been uninterrupted for centuries. The Jewish community of Milan was born from the already vibrant Mantuan community. The first Jew, Abramo ibn Ezra, arrived in Mantua in 1145. The community increased over the years until it reached its peak in 1600. There were 6,000 Jews living in the city in that year. The Jews were artisans, merchants, businessmen, and moneylenders. They were also close to the Courts, as personal physicians to the Duke. Some Jews were musicians, such as Salamone Rossi, while others were authors of comedies and actors, such as Leone de 'Sommi and one of his sisters, "Madame Europa."

Even though the Jews were protected by the Gonzaga family, they did not have an easy life. They had to wear the special marking identifying them as Jews and in 1612, were forced to live in a ghetto. In 1708, Austria captured the Duchy of Mantua. The restrictions placed on the Jews were now abolished. It was not until 1789, however, that Napoleon dismantled the ghetto. Jews were now permitted to attend public schools. They were no longer subjected to pay the tariffs that had been paid to the sovereigns for centuries. Leopold II conceded complete equality to the Jews.

Many Jews in Mantua participated in the *Risorgimento.* Giuseppi Finzi, a native of Rivarolo, and the writer, Tullio Masaranti were among the martyrs. The Jewish community diminished in importance after the unification of Italy. In 1931, there were 669 Jews in the city. During World War II, forty Jews were deported. Today, there are 160 Jews in Mantua.

BOZZOLO

ANCIENT SYNAGOGUE Via Bonoldi #10

MANTUA (Mantova)

GHETTO SITE Via Giuseppe Bertani

The four gateways to the ghetto were located at Via Giustiziati, Piazza Concordia, Via Spagnoli, and Via Bertani. Following a plague and the sacking of the city in 1630, the area of the ghetto was diminished and the gate which closed Via Bertani was removed.

There were six synagogues located within the ghetto; three followed the Italian ritual and three followed the German ritual. There were no synagogues for the other rituals, although there were many Franco-Provençal Jews. The gates of the ghetto were torn down in 1798.

The former German ritual synagogues were located on the corner of Via Spagnoli, in the Piazza Concordia. They were built between 1588-95. The Italian ritual synagogues were located at Via Bertani and Via Scuola Grande. The Norsa Torrazzo Synagogue and the Grand Italian Synagogue were built in 1513. The first was demolished but faithfully reconstructed on Via Govi #11 at the turn of this century. The other synagogue was demolished in 1938. Its furnishings were sent to the Ponivez Yeshiva in B'nai B'raq, in Israel. The third Italian ritual synagogue was known as the Cases Synagogue and was located at Via Bertani and Via San Francesca da Paola. It was destroyed in 1929. Its furnishings were sent to the Haychal Shlomo, the Rabbinical Seat, in Jerusalem.

The former Rabbinical Seat of Mantua was located at Via Bertani #54. The façade is adorned with panels designed with imaginative images of biblical cities.

CHURCH of VITTORIO

Via Madonna della Vittorio and Via Domenico Farnelli

Daniele Norsa, a prominent banker, purchased a house at this site in 1496. It is said that there was a likeness of the Madonna on the façade of the house. Norsa erased the image, after receiving permission from the the ecclesiastical authorities. The image was suitably compensated for with money. The citizens of Mantua, however, were furious. In order to placate their anger, the Marquis

1795 Ark from Mantua now located in the Beit Yeshayahu Synagogue in Tel Aviv, Israel.

The Great Italian Synagogue of Mantua.

Francesca Gonzaga ordered Norsa to demolish his home and build, at his own expense, the Cathedral of Santa Maria della Vittorio.

The episode is memorialized by an anonymous painter from the Montegna school. The artist depicts the Madonna della Vittorio holding a model of the church which was built on the site of Norsa's home. The Jews are portrayed at the bottom of the painting. They are all wearing the special identification marking on their clothing, the yellow circle.

The Norsa family (at bottom of painting, wearing circle ID markings) was forced to build a church. A model of that church is held by the priest.

SYNAGOGUE and COMMUNITY CENTER

Via Govi #11 Tel. (0376) 321 490

The synagogue archives contain documents from 1522-1810. There are civil registers from 1750, administrative archives from 1910, ten *ketubot,* the archives of the *Jewish Civil Tribune,* and manuscript letters sent from 19th century musicians. A precious and highly detailed manuscript,the *Moreh Nevuchim,* by Maimonides, dated 1349, has been in the Norsa family's possession for centuries.

The Norsa Synagogue is located in the courtyard of the main synagogue at Via Govi #11. This small synagogue is a splendid replica of the original Norsa Torrazzo Synagogue. The furnishings date from the 1700s. There are stuccoworks which cover the walls. They exalt the magnificence of the Norsa family and quote passages from the Bible. This synagogue is only used on major Jewish holidays.

The Norsa Synagogue.

Italian Synagogue in Jerusalem houses the 1543 Ark from Mantua-Sermide.

JEWISH CEMETERY Via Legnano

The first Jewish cemetery was located at Via del Gradaro. Today, it is the site of military barracks. The present cemetery is located on Via Legnano, just beyond the old wall of the city.

MILAN (Milano)

In 1840, there were 200 Jews living in the City of Milan. It was still part of the community of Mantua. In 1866, the Jewish community of Milan outnumbered the mother-community of Mantua and broke away. The flourishing commerce, extraordinary economic and industrial growth, and the cosmopolitan climate caused the city to accept its Jewish community with tolerance and respect. There were 2,000 Jews in 1890, out of a total population of 400,000.

The first synagogue was located in the apartment of Rabbi Prospero Moise Ariani. It was located at Via Stampa #4. This congregation closed when the new synagogue on Via Guastalla was built.

The Jewish Community Center of Milan was located at Via Amedei #9 during the 1920s and 1930s. The Jewish population of Milan swelled from 4,500 in the 1920s to over 12,000 during the late 1930s. When Hitler came to power, many Jews came from Germany and other parts of Italy. In 1940, 5,000 fled from the city.

In 1939, the Jewish Relief Organization, *Delasem*, was located at Viale Vittorio Veneto #12. This building was destroyed during the bombings in 1943. The Jewish Rest Home on Via Ippolito Nievo was also destroyed during this raid. The elderly and the sick were removed from this location in 1942 and were sent to the old hospital in Mantua. The Nazis deported forty of these people. Only three returned after the war.

During the war, 896 Jews were deported. Only 50 returned. After the war, the Jews used the Palazzo Odeschalchi on Via Unione #5 for their synagogue services and communal needs. That building was used by the Antonio Sciesa Fascist group during the war. The building was used until the new synagogue was completed in 1953.

Milan became the center for clandestine emigration to Palestine. The headquarters of the Palestine Brigade Club was located at Via Cantu #5. Yehudah Arazi (Alon) led the *Aliyah Bet* and organized departures of refugees from several Italian ports in 1946. Jews were trained in field exercises and in the use of weapons.

The Jewish population of Milan is approximately 7,500. The Jewish community consists of Jews from fifteen countries. The most prevalent groups are from Iran, Egypt, and Libya.

SYNAGOGUE Via Guastalla #19 Tel. (01) 791 851

The Jewish community commissioned architect Luca Beltrami, noted for his new Permanente Building and the restoration of the Sforzesco Castle. The synagogue was inaugurated on September 28, 1892. The most important and influential citizens attended the opening ceremonies. The design of the synagogue was eclectic.

In August, 1943, the synagogue was almost completely destroyed during an aerial bombing attack. Only the front façade of the building and a wing housing the synagogue offices were left standing. The synagogue was reconstructed following the war. Architects Manfredo d'Urbino and Eugenio Gentili Tedeschi designed a new edifice behind the original front façade. The Italian government allocated 75 million Lire, over a 30-year period, for the reconstruction of the synagogue. This sum covered only half of the overall cost of the work. The work was completed in 1953.

The Ark is designed with large dark red marble slabs. The doors are covered with gold leaf. The Tevah has been placed in the center of the hall. Its baluster is made of red marble from Candoglio and is supported by black lacquered steel and bronze pillars. The Tevah is illuminated by a large dome-shaped chandelier. There are four large brushed-brass light fixtures suspended above the pulpit area. The walls in the sanctuary are a neutral color. The floor is designed with red and pink marble. The columns supporting the women's gallery are pink granite.

The basement of the synagogue contains a small chapel which is used by eastern Sephardic Jews. The furnishings in this chapel are from the former synagogue of Sermide. The Carlo and Gianna Shapira School is located on the ground floor of the adjoining office complex. The furnishings are from the former synagogue of Fiorenzuola, a community in Emilia Romagna. The rabbinical offices are housed in this wing of the synagogue complex.

JEWISH CEMETERIES

A stone tablet on the wall of the San Francesco d'Assisi al Foppolino Church, located at Via Paolo Giovio #11, records the site of the first Jewish cemetery, which was established in 1808. The present cemetery is located behind Viale Certosa, in Musocco. The writer Sabatino Lopez, is buried here. There is an additional section located in the Monumentale Cemetery, on Viale Ceresio.

CENTER for the DOCUMENTATION of CONTEMPORARY JUDAISM

Via Eupili #8 Tel. 310 692 or 316 338

This institution collects documents and books on contemporary Judaism. It contains an historical archive, newspaper and periodical library with 641 titles, and a specialized library with more than 10,000 volumes. The principal sections of research material include: events and problems of the Jews of Italy and throughout the world, anti-Semitism, deportation and extermination, Jewish religion and culture, Zionism, and the State of Israel. The institute is open to the public Monday through Friday, from 8:50 a.m. to 12:15 p.m. The adjoining villas once housed the Hebrew school.

SALLY MAYER HEBREW SCHOOL Via Sally Mayer #4/6 Tel. 416 270

This complex was completed in 1964. It is attended by 750 children, from pre-school to high school. The building contains all of the modern facilities such as a gymnasium, library, labs, and a cafeteria. There is a small chapel used by eastern Sephardic Jews. The furnishings in this chapel are from the former synagogue in Mantua.

G. GUASTALLA and M. BATTINO REST HOME

Via Leone XIII #1 Tel. 496 331

This large complex was built in 1973 and was designed by architects Yonathan De Paz and Donato d'Urbino. This modern facility contains a small chapel and a kosher dining room. Meals are available to the public, only by prior arrangement.

OTHER SYNAGOGUES:

Beth Medrash Beth Shlomo–Chabad *Via U. Foscolo 3-Galleria Vittorio Emannuel*
Tempio Centrale *Via Guastalla 19 Tel. (2) 551-2101*
Ohel Jaakov *Via Cellini 2 Tel. 545-5076*
Beth Shlomo *Corso di Porta Romana 3*
Chabad *Via F. Bronzetti 18 Tel. (2) 7010-0080*
Angelo Donati Beth Hamedrash *Via Sally Mayer 4 Tel. 415-1660*
Oratorio di Via Jommelli 18 *Tel. 236-504*
Oratorio Sfardita *Via delle Tuberose 14 Tel. 415-1660*
Oratorio di Via Eupili 8
Oratorio Nuovo Residenza per Anziana *Via Leone XII #1*

KOSHER PROVISIONS:

Beth Medrash Beth Shlomo–Chabad *Via U. Foscolo 3*
This small synagogue and cafe is housed in the center of the world-renowned Milano Galleria Vittorio Emannuel in the center of town. It is located between La Scala Opera House and the Duomo. The congre - gation was formed in 1940 in the concentration camp located in Ferramonti (Calabria) The camp was liberated in 1943. After the war ended, Milan was the center of Aliath Beth, which was organized to bring Holocaust survivors to Israel legally or illegally. While awaiting transportation to Israel, the Jews organized Congregation Sherit Aplita (The Rest of the Remnants). The shul was located at Via Unione 5. The Ark from that congregation was incorporated in this new shul in the Galleria Vittorio Emannuel.
Carmel Pizza *viale San Gimignano 10 Tel. (2) 416-368*
Restaurant Giovannino *Via A. Sciesa 8 Tel. 551-95-582*
Eretz Grocery *Largo Scalabrini 5 Tel. 423-6891*

JEWISH BOOKSTORES:

LIBRERIA PIAZZA SAN BABILA Corso Monforte #2 Tel. 799 219

LIBRERIA CLAUDIANA Via F. Sforza #12/a Tel. 791 518

RESEARCH LIBRARIES:

AMBROSIANA Piazza Pio XI #2

NAZIONALE BRAIDENSA Via Brera #28

COMUNALE CENTRALE Corso di Porta Vittorio #6

MILAN STATE ARCHIVE Via Senato #10

HISTORICAL ARCHIVE (Castello Sforzesco) Piazza Castello

OSTIANO

GOVERNOR'S HOUSE

The Governor's House is located in the courtyard of the Gonzaga Castle. A small group of Jews lived in these quarters. The furnishings of the synagogue, which was built in 1700, have vanished. If you wish to visit, contact Mrs. Caterina Regonini De Pizzol at (0372) 85177. The ancient Jewish cemetery is located in Montagnetta.

POMPONESCO

SYNAGOGUE SITE Via Cantoni #15

This former synagogue is now used as a storage area for the Cafe Sport. There is a bust in front of the City Hall and a street named for the Cantoni family. Alberto Cantoni was a Jewish writer and a local hero. He died in 1904.

RIVAROLO MANTOVANO

ANCIENT SYNAGOGUE Piazza Giuseppe Finzi

The former synagogue was sold to the Mutual Aid Association of Rivarolese Workers in 1903. That group covered the original Hebrew inscriptions with inscriptions of their own. A portrait of Garibaldi was placed on the spot which once housed the Holy Ark. There is an inscription thanking the Rivarolese people. The building is presently owned by the Cafe Diana. The former synagogue is located in the back of the bar and up a flight of stairs.

Rivarolo Mantovano Synagogue.

JEWISH CEMETERIES

The first cemetery was located at Via Cavour, near the Porta Brescia. This cemetery was discovered during construction of a building on the site. The two tombstones have been removed and placed in the local tourist office. The 19th century cemetery was located at Porta Mantova, just outside the city walls.

SABBIONETA

ANCIENT SYNAGOGUE Via B. Campi

The furnishings of this former synagogue have been sent to a synagogue in Mantua. This city was famous for its Jewish printers. The street, *Via della Stamperia,* memorializes these Jewish printers. The first edition of the *Mirkevet ha-Mishneh,* by Isaac ben Judah Abrabanel (1437-1508), was printed by Tobia Foa and his sons.

Sabbioneta Synagogue.

CHURCH of INCORONATA

There is a stone tablet located under the portico of this church. It records the grand gesture of the Jew, Leone Donato Forti. In 1826, he rescued this church for the "love of his country." This church had been desecrated by Napoleon's troops. The large villa on Via Accademia, with its ornate doors and coats of arm, belonged to the Forti family.

SONCINO

Soncino is found in the Province of Cremona. It was famous as a center of Jewish printing. The Da Spira family, Israel Nathan and his son Joshua Shlomo, came from the City of Speyer, on the Rhine River, in 1484. Israel Nathan was a doctor and a rabbi. He obtained a license to print books in Hebrew and Latin from the Sforza family. The printing house soon became one of the most prestigious establishments of the time.

When the Jews were forced to leave the Duchy, various members of the family split up, yet continued printing. They established printing houses in Casalmaggiore, Pesaro, Brescia, Naples, Rimini, Istanbul, and Cairo. They assumed the surname *Soncino,* to remember their first "home."

There is a small museum in Soncino, called the House of the Printers, *Casa degli Stampatori.* This is where the printers worked for nearly a century. For further information, contact the local tourist board at (0374) 85050 or the Municipal Building at 85516.

Note: There is a kosher salami factory at Via Cavagne #6.

VIADANA

SYNAGOGUE SITE Via Bonomi #29

There were two synagogues located at this site. The small synagogue was located at #29. At #31, an unfinished synagogue still stands empty. It was commissioned by the Jewish community in the early 1800s. Architect Casalasco Carlo Visioli was to design this new synagogue, regardless of its cost! It had a circular floor plan, eight tall columns, and a large windowed cupola. There was to be a gallery for the women. The synagogue was never completed. Some say that it exceeded the needs of the community. The large synagogue remained empty until the end of World War II. The Jewish community became extinct following the war. It was then purchased by the Marcheselli family. The space has been converted into a carpentry shop.

Medieval painting of King David's Psalms.

Cortina d'Ampezzo
Auronzo
MARMOLADA 3343
ANTELAU 3263
PASSO DE MAURIA 1295
Pieve di Cadore
S. Martino di Castrozza
Longarone
Gosaldo
Belluno
Feltre
M. ORTIGARA 2105
Asiago
Arten
Malcesine
M. BALDO 2200
M. PASUBIO 2235
Lago
Follina
Pederobba
Vittorio Veneto
Schio
Bassano d. Grappa
Conegliano
Giazza
Thiene
Asolo
Valdagno
Breganze
Montebelluna
Grezzana
Sandrigo
Oderzo
Verona
Arzignano
Vicenza
Castelfranco Veneto
Treviso
Soave
Portogruaro
Scorze
Padova (Padua)
Noale
S. Dona di Piave
Isola d. Scala
Lonigo
Mestre
Eraclea
Venézia (Venice)
Abano Terme
Mira
Minerbe
Montegrotto Terme
Lido di Jesolo
Nogara
Este
Legnaro
Lido
Legnago
Monselice
Badia Polesine
Chioggia
Lendinara
Rovigo
Cavarzere
Ficarolo
Loreo
Adria
Contarina
Porto Tolle

Veneto Region

Venice became the capital of the entire Veneto region in the 15th century through a series of wars and conquests. The "Lion" of St. Mark dominated a vast territory on the Italian mainland and imposed its laws and its economic policies.

The Jews were generally protected by the Serene. As merchants, the Jews were able to assure money to the state treasuries. They were experienced in trade and had many international contacts. Venice was a cosmopolitan city and was tolerant in religious matters. It would accept diverse thoughts, as long as they did not go against the city's own interests. Jews were therefore able to develop their own businesses. They lived throughout the entire region. They lived in the large cities of Venice, Padua, and Verona. They also lived in the small rural areas and often practiced moneylending. These moneylenders were often the only Jews in town. There were many small Jewish centers in the vicinity of Padua. There are ancient Jewish cemeteries in Este, Monselice, and Montagna. There were small synagogues in Cittadella and Conselve, however, no trace of them remains.

In the northeastern part of Veneto, great catastrophes befell the Jewish communities. In 1547, the synagogue and Jewish cemetery in Asolo (near Trevise) were destroyed in a sacking of the city. There are still two Jewish tombstones built into the Piazza of Asolo. The 16th century synagogue in Soave (near Verona) is recalled only in the name of the street, *Contrada degli ebrei.* The Jews were expelled from Vicenza and Bassano between 1500 and 1550. These were fairly large Jewish settlements. These expulsions fomented by the anti-Jewish predication of Bernard of Feltre and the ritual murder trial in Trent. The Jews sought havens in more "protected" communities. Sometimes these havens were permanent, but too often, they were only temporary.

CASTLEFRANCO VENETO

GIORGIONE MUSEUM Piazza San Liberale

This art museum is where one of the greatest Renaissance masters, Giorgione, lived and worked. Some have said that Giorgione was of Jewish descent. The basis for this is the fact that Giorgione was excluded from the public market, which is a matter of religious bias. We do not have a surname for Giorgione. We only know his place of origin. In the 1500s, Jews did not have surnames. Giorgione was also an accomplished musician. Music was an important part of the education of children from wealthy Jewish families. The Jews of the Veneto region were doctors, moneylenders, and teachers of music and dance.

The relationship between Italian art and Jewish art followed very precise rules, from the Common Era to the Emancipation. Jews were kept out of the greater arts such as painting, sculpture, and architecture. Jews entered into Italian art as objects of representation. They were depicted as wicked beings in the Christological story or were shown as authors of supposed evil deeds connected to the Hagiographic stories.

CONEGLIANO

GHETTO SITE Via Caronelli

Jews arrived in Conegliano in 1398 and remained here for over five hundred years. In 1637, the Venetian Republic ordered the Jews to live in a ghetto. The first ghetto was located on the Contrada di Siletto. A synagogue, following the Ashkenazic ritual, was built. In 1675, the Jews were forced to move to the Contrada del Ruio, their second ghetto. The furnishings from the first synagogue were transferred to the new ghetto.

The Jews in the Veneto region were involved in the silk trade. They had factories and spinning mills in the ghetto and in the surrounding countryside. It seems that the Jews introduced this trade into the region. In 1866, the ghetto walls were dismantled. Marco Grassini, a prominent Jew, was elected mayor of the city.

The furnishings from the synagogue of Conegliano Veneto were shipped to the Italian Synagogue in Jerusalem, Israel.

ANCIENT SYNAGOGUE Via Caronelli #17

The synagogue was built inside the tallest building of the ghetto. Its Ark was taken from the first ghetto in the city. It was gold-plated and designed in Baroque style. It was donated by the Grassini family. The Austrian army occupied the city during World War I. The Hungarian military chaplain, Rabbi Deutsch, celebrated Yom Kippur services in this synagogue. The synagogue thereafter, went into disuse. When the last Jew in Conegliano, Adolfo Vital, died in 1944, the Community Council of Venice granted permission to transfer the

Conegliano Veneto Bimah, now housed in Jerusalem.

synagogue furnishings to Israel. In 1949, the Synagogue of Conegliano was rebuilt in Jerusalem. It is located in the Italian Synagogue, at Rechov Hillel #27.

JEWISH CEMETERY Via San Giuseppe

The original cemetery is located near the Church of Madonna del Carmine. The oldest tombstones bear the family crests; the squirrel of the Coneian family, the lion of the Grassini family, the cock of the Luzzatto family, and the dove of the Parente family. In 1880, a Jewish section was inaugurated in the community cemetery.

MESTRE

SYNAGOGUE Via Giose Borsi #28

Services are held on Friday evenings.

PADUA (Padova)

The first Jews arrived in Padua around the year 1000. In 1298, a certain Jacopo Bonacossi, a gifted doctor and translator of the famous text of Averroe, moved to Padua. Many Jews attended the Rabbinical Academy and Medical School. The University of Padua was the only one in Europe which accepted Jewish students during the middle 1300s. The Jewish students, however, had to pay twice as much tuition for this privilege. They also had to present the University with 170 pounds of candy before they could graduate. This custom stopped in the 1700s. There were 80 Jewish graduates from the Medical School between 1517 and 1619. Between 1619 and 1721, there were 149 graduates.

During the period of the Commune and the rule of the Carraresi family, the Jews settled between Borgo Savonardo and the Ponte Molino. They organized the first synagogue and established the first cemetery. In 1405, Padua fell under the rule of the Venetian Republic. The Jews were required to sell all of their homes and properties. They were required to reduce the amount of interest on loans from 25 to 12 percent. In protest, the Jews closed all of their banks. Ultimately, the decrees were rescinded. In 1492, the Jews suffered severely with the establishment of the Christian-run *Monte di Pieta* pawn shops. Michele of Milan, a minor priest, preached violent anti-Semitic sermons.

In 1509, the troops of Maximilian of Hapsburg entered Padua. The Jewish quarters were sacked. When the Venetians drove the Austrians from the city, the Jewish areas were again sacked, this time, by the Venetians. From 1509 to 1560, July 17 was celebrated as a victory of the Venetians over the Austrians. Three major races were held as part of the celebration; the race of the whores, the race of the asses, and the race of the Jews. The Jews were forced to run between the crowds of people, from Ponte Molino to Piaza della Signoria. A record of this event remains in a painting which hangs in the Palazzo Schifanoia, in Ferrara.

In 1525, the Jewish community inaugurated its first Ashkenazic synagogue on Via delle Piazza. A second congregation, following the Italian ritual, was built in

1548 and was located at Via Martino and Via Solferino. A third synagogue, following the Spanish ritual, was built in 1617 and was located on Via San Martino and Via Solferino.

The ghetto was established in 1601. It extended from Via dei Fabbri, Via Urbana, Via Sirena, Via dell 'Arco and went as far as the Via Spirito Santo. The ghetto was closed with gates at four points. There were two guards at each gate. One Christian guard stood outside the ghetto and one Jewish guard stood within the ghetto walls. The streets of the ghetto were narrow. The houses were unsanitary. During the plague of 1631, 421 of the 721 inhabitants of the ghetto died. This was the highest recorded mortality rate among Jews in the history of an epidemic.

Many Paduan Jews established industries outside of the city. In 1645, the Trieste family had a silk factory in Abano, which employed 600 people. Salomon Alpron had 200 looms in the City of Brugine in 1751. During this same period, the Trieste, Landi, Salomon, and Romano families employed over 5,000 people and produced 100,000 bolts of silk a year.

Paduan Jews were often forced to listen to sermons in the Church degli Eremitani (until 1715). The first conversion to Christianity was the most sensational. In 1601, Rabbi Salone Cattelan took the Christian name of Prosdocimo.

The Jews have celebrated acts of salvation when the ghetto was spared from being burned. This was called the *Purim of Fire*. The *Purim of Buda* occurred when the Jews were saved from destruction after they were accused of committing acts of cruelty against Christians during the Siege of Budapest.

The doors of the ghetto were torn down in 1797. The French, however, were later driven out by the Austrians. The Jews who remained in the ghetto area were attacked by the locals who accused them of helping the French. The Congress of Vienna (1814) assigned the regions of Veneto, Lombardy, and Trentino to Austria. A few illuminating laws were introduced. Elementary education was now mandatory. This law did not have an effect on the Jews since the illiteracy rate in the ghetto was only 6 percent, compared to the general illiteracy rate of 50 percent in the overall population.

Padua was always an important center for Jewish studies since the 1400s. From 1829, Padua housed the Superior Rabbinical Academy (later known as the Rabbinical College), where David Luzzatto and Lelio Della Torre lectured. The

Holy Ark of the Tempio Grande, presently housed in the Yad Eliyahu Synagogue in Tel Aviv, Israel.

Rabbinical College was moved to Rome in 1870.

There were 1,378 Jews living in Padua in 1881. During the Second World War, 46 Jews were deported. Today, there are approximately 200 Jews in Padua.

ANCIENT SYNAGOGUE Via San Martino and Via Solferino

The oldest synagogue was created in 1525. It belonged to an Ashkenazic group. It was transformed in 1683 and again in 1892. In 1892, however, the transformation was radical. It became an Italian ritual congregation. The 17th century Bimah in the center of the room was removed. The furnishings and decorations were left intact. In 1927, the building was damaged by fire. In 1943, the Fascists threw a firebomb through the roof, and completely destroyed it. Only the marble Ark was spared. In 1955, the Ark was shipped to Israel. It was reassembled in the Yad Eliyahu Synagogue, in Tel Aviv.

The Spanish ritual synagogue was located in the same building as the Italian congregation. It is entered from Via della Piazza #14. It was inaugurated in 1617, in the house of Michelino della Bella. The hall measures 14 x 4.9 meters. This synagogue is not designed in the typical floor plan of ghetto synagogues. The Ark and Tevah are on opposite walls, however, they are located on the long walls. The synagogue was closed in 1892 when the different rituals were united into only one congregation. The furnishings of this synagogue have been sent to the Haychal Shlomo, the Seat of the Rabbinate, in Jerusalem.

GREAT ITALIAN SYNAGOGUE Via San Martino and Via Solferino #9

This synagogue was organized in 1548 by Rabbi Jochanan Treves, Aron Salom di Mordecai Rava, and Moise de Roman. The synagogue has undergone many restorations. In 1892, all of the different rituals were merged into this congregation. The synagogue was closed only during World War II. The synagogue measures 18 x 7 meters. Its monumental Ark and tall Tevah face each other from the middle of the longer walls, dividing the hall in two. The Ark was carved from a plane tree which was knocked down by a lightning bolt, in the 16th century.

RABBINICAL ACADEMY SITE Via San Martino e Solferino and Via Arco

The former Rabbinical Academy is presently owned by the Toscanelli Hotel. The ghetto "skyscrapers" are still standing along Via Arco. Additional floors were added onto the original buildings in order to accommodate the hundreds of Jews who were forced into this ghetto area.

JEWISH CEMETERIES

The oldest Jewish cemetery dates back to 1384. It is located near San Leonardo. The tomb of Rabbi Katzenellenbogen (1482-1565), known as the *Maharam* of Padua, is located in this cemetery. The tombstone has an emblem of a crouching cat (*katze* means cat in German). Many eastern European Jews make pilgrimages to the tomb of this saintly rabbi.

The second cemetery was created in 1450. It is located in Via Codalunga, near the Bastione della Gatta. The celebrated Isaac ben Yehuda Abrabanel (1437-1508) is buried here. Abrabanel was the Minister of Finance for King Alphonse V of Portugal, and then for King Ferdinand of Spain. His son, who lived in Venice during those years, had him buried in this cemetery. The cemetery was devastated in 1509 by Austrian troops. It is no longer in use and was left in the custody of the nearby Sisters of Santa Maria Materdomini. Some of the tombstones are kept in the Civic Museum.

There is another cemetery located at Via Sorio #124, near the Porta San Giovanni. Samuel David Luzzatto (1800-1866) is buried here. The tomb of Dante Lattes is also in this cemetery. The caretaker of this cemetery can be contacted at (049) 30577.

Heychal Shlomo Synagogue in Jerusalem houses the Ark and Bimah from the Tempio Spagnolo of Padua.

ROVIGO

GHETTO SITE Piazza Umberto Merlin

A street in Rovigo has been named in memory of the Jewish poetess Argia Castiglione Vitalis.

ANCIENT SYNAGOGUE Via Corridoni #18

The furnishings from this former synagogue were sent to the synagogue in Padua.

JEWISH CEMETERY Via Stacche

The original Jewish cemetery, from the 1500s, was located on Via Mure Soccorso. It is completely abandoned. The present cemetery is located on Via Stacche. For further information, call Elvira Consigli at (0423) 28385.

TREVISO

ANCIENT SYNAGOGUE Portico Oscuro #11

The first Jews arrived in 905. The city was noted for its great yeshiva. Aharon Abu al Rabbi, author of the "Commentary on Rashi," studied in Treviso. In 1480, the Jews in the neighboring town of Portobuffole were accused of ritual murder and were burned alive in the Piazza of Venice. The Jews of Treviso were accused of helping Maximilian of Hapsburg defeat Venice at Agnedello in 1509. Their homes were destroyed by the angry mobs and the Jews were then driven out of the city.

JEWISH CEMETERY Vicolo San Lazzaro

The old 15th century cemetery at Borgo Cavour, was discovered during excavation work in 1880. Those tombstones have been kept in the local museum. The modern Jewish cemetery dates from the 19th century.

VENICE (Venezia)

The first documents that mention Jews in Venice are from 945 and 992. The Venetian Senate prohibited ship captains, who were heading for the Orient, from accepting Jewish crew-members. There were several Jews from Germany and the Near East who were living in Venice. They were merchants and moneylenders. They were granted special permission to live in the city, which had to be renewed each year.

In 1394, the Venetian Republic imposed the identification marking. Jews were required to wear a yellow circle on their cloaks. This was later changed to a yellow hat (1496) and again changed, in 1500, to a red hat.

In 1509, Venice lost much of its mainland in the defeat by the Cambrai League in Agnadello. Thousands of refugees took refuge in Venice. They were fleeing the Lansquenets of Maximilian of Hapsburg. Many Jews who, until then, lived in the area between Vicenza and Conegliano, entered the city. They were particularly maltreated by the German troops.

When the war ended, Venice wanted to get rid of its thousands of refugees, including the Jewish refugees. The Senate knew how important the Jewish merchants were to the future economy of the city, and decided to approach the situation in a different manner. It decided to separate the Jews from the rest of the population and placed them in a separate quarter, the ghetto. Some say that the term *ghetto* is derived from the German word *gitter*, a grating or iron bars. Some say that the term is derived from the Hebrew word *get*, which means divorce. Others say that the word is from the German word *gasse*, an alleyway. Whatever its origin, the word quickly became synonymous with forced segregation and separation, particularly for Jews.

On March 29, 1516, seven hundred Jews of German and Italian origin, were forced to move to the island of the Ghetto Nuovo. It was located in the northwest part of the city. It was a peripheral and unsanitary area. It was near the jails and the Convent of San Girolamo. Churchmen were responsible for burying executed prisoners.

When the island was designated for the Jews, it was already partially inhabited. These people were forced to leave the island in order to make room for the newcomers. Rents were increased by a third. The two bridges of Rio San Girolamo and Rio del Ghetto were fitted with gates. The Jews had to pay the guards who closed these gates at sunset and reopened them at dawn. There were additional guards who patrolled the canals in boats during the evenings.

The German and Italian Jews were enclosed in the ghetto in 1516. The Levantine Jews remained free until 1541. The Jews from Spain, Portugal, and western Italy remained free until 1589. These last two groups were enclosed in the Ghetto Vecchio (old ghetto). In 1603, the German Jews were assigned to the newest ghetto, Ghetto Nuovissimo.

The space available to each group immediately became insufficient. Several hundred Jews lived in 7,000 square meters, of which 3,000 square meters were fields. The situation worsened as the years passed and families grew. In order to accommodate all of these people, houses were subdivided. They were split up into small sections so that every nook and cranny was utilized. Additional floors were added onto existing structures. Sometimes they were as high as nine stories and were known as 16th century "skyscrapers."

Passageways were designed between each house in the ghetto. They linked all of the houses, synagogues, and meeting places. Each group built its own synagogue within these "barracks" of the ghetto. They were camouflaged on the outside and simple in structure and furnishings on the inside. Over the years, these synagogues were embellished with finely sculpted furnishings, polished silver, chandeliers, silk tapestries, and brocaded drapes. There was, in a sense, a competition between the groups. They lived elbow to elbow, yet maintained separate rituals and traditions.

The ghetto was a commercial center, not only for Jews and foreigners, but also for the Christians. Every morning, when the gates of the ghetto were opened, hundreds of Christians poured into its streets. In the beginning of the 17th century, the political and economic power of the Serene began to decay. The wars against the Turks bled its resources, and the great geographic discoveries moved the axis of trade from the Mediterranean to the Atlantic. Venice became a peripheral economic and financial center. Inevitably, the Jewish community also began to decline. Many Jews moved elsewhere. The population of the ghettos dropped from 5,000 to 1,500.

The fiscal pressure placed on the Jewish community by the authorities of the Republic, however, did not diminish. The Jews were forced to pay the same amount of tax. They still had to pay the same amount of rent, even though many of the houses were unoccupied. In 1735, the community failed.

The doors of the ghetto were torn down in 1796, with the arrival of Napoleon. The wealthy families left the ghettos, while the poorer families remained. The Jews obtained equal rights under Napoleonic rule (1805-14). The Revolution of 1848 was headed by Daniele Manin, a Venetian Jew. The history of the Venetian Jews became similar to that of their co-religionists throughout Italy after the annexation of the Veneto region by the Kingdom of Italy in 1866. The Jewish community began to decline. In 1931, the community had 1,814 members.

During World War II, 205 Jews were deported, including the Chief Rabbi of the community, Adolfo Ottolenghi. There were only 1,050 Jews left in Venice following the war. Many moved to Mestre or to the large cities. Today, there are about 630 Jews in Venice.

VENICE GHETTO

The ghetto of Venice was the first in Europe. It has preserved its original appearance since it was instituted in 1516.

To find the ghetto, walk out of the railroad terminal and turn left, onto the Lista de Spagna. Continue until the first canal. Cross over the bridge, the Ponte delle Guglia, and immediately turn left. Proceed about 300 feet until the entrance of the ghetto. There is a small yellow sign which says, "To the Synagogues," in Italian, English, and Hebrew. This is the entrance to the Ghetto Vecchio.

The hinges which held the gates of the ghetto are still visible on the sides of the main entrance to the Ghetto Vecchio. There are two bricked-up windows on either side of the narrow passageway. Theses were the check-points where the guards monitored all people who entered and left the ghetto. The Ghetto Vecchio was instituted for the Levantine and western Italian Jews in 1541. This narrow passageway was the "main street" of the ghetto. It contained a fruit store, butcher, bakery, pharmacy, candy store, cafe, and a hotel.

There is a memorial plaque on the left wall. This records the regulations for the closing of the ghetto gates and the penalties levied against transgressors. The building above this passageway once housed the Talmud Torah of the western Jews. The first open plaza in this ghetto is called the Campiello delle Scuole. The Spanish and Levantine synagogues are located in this square.

SPANISH SYNAGOGUE (Scola)

The Spanish Scola was built in 1555 by Spanish and *marrano* Jews. It was restored in 1635, perhaps by Baldassarre Longhena, and transformed again at

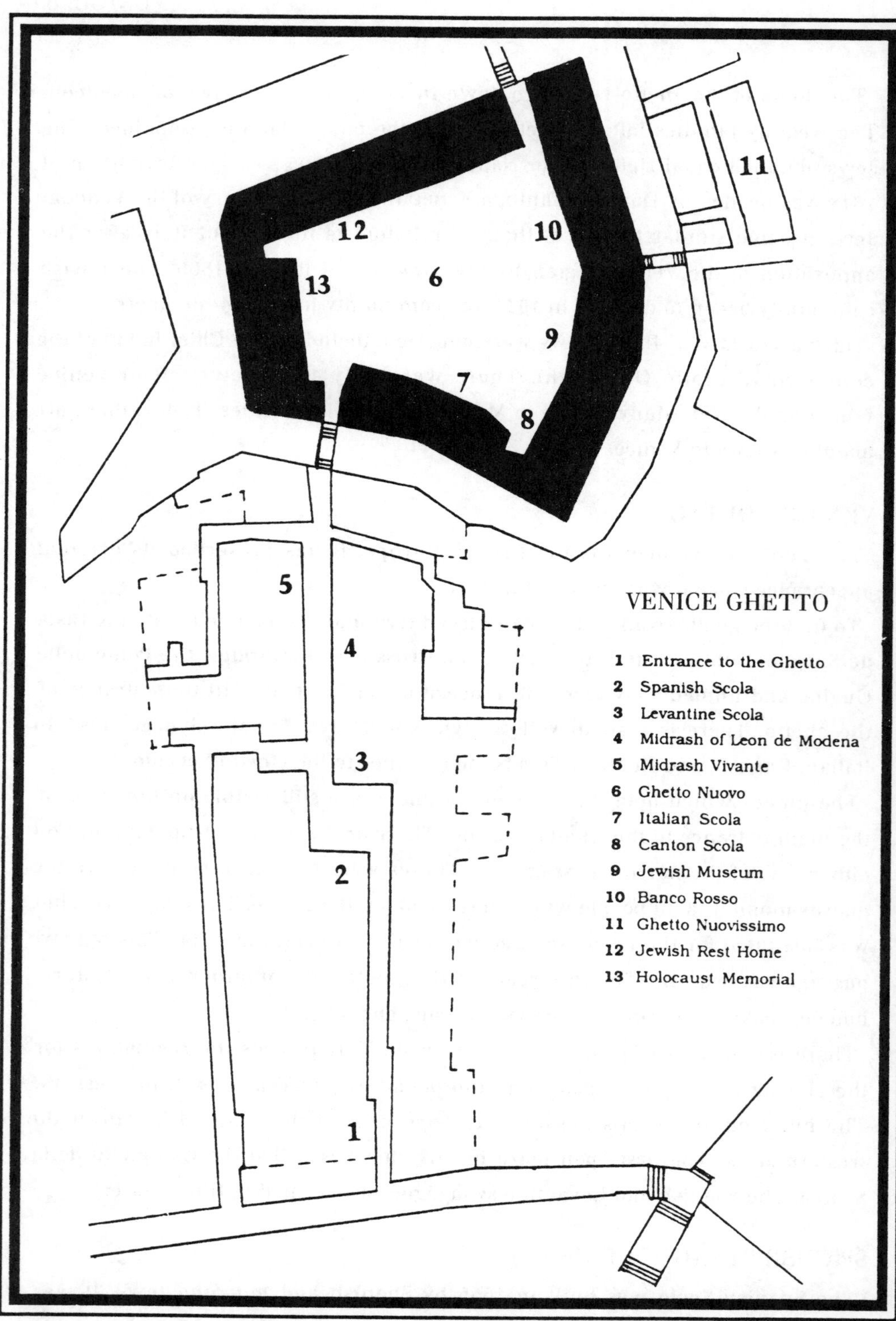
11
12
10
13
6
9
7
8
5
4
3
2
1
VENICE GHETTO
1 Entrance to the Ghetto
2 Spanish Scola
3 Levantine Scola
4 Midrash of Leon de Modena
5 Midrash Vivante
6 Ghetto Nuovo
7 Italian Scola
8 Canton Scola
9 Jewish Museum
10 Banco Rosso
11 Ghetto Nuovissimo
12 Jewish Rest Home
13 Holocaust Memorial

the end of the 19th century. The Community of Venice and the Superintendent of Environmental and Architectural Goods are presently restoring the women's gallery and the supporting pillars of the hall. The synagogue is open on the Sabbath and on major Jewish holidays (during the spring, summer, and fall). Tours of this synagogue are available through the Jewish Museum of Venice.

There is a memorial plaque on the front façade of the building which is dedicated to the Jews who were deported during the last war. The vestibule contains a set of doors on the left which lead into a small Talmud Torah. There is also an exquisite chapel which is no longer utilized. The stairs on the right side of the vestibule lead up to the main sanctuary.

The sanctuary measures 22 x 13 meters. The Ark and Tevah are at opposite ends of the hall. The central space of the hall remains empty. This was customary in all of the synagogues of Venice. The Classical-Baroque Ark is flanked by two dark marble Corinthian columns. A semicircular wooden baluster encloses a dais with two steps. The lectern of the officient is located on this dais. This transformation occurred at the end of the 19th century. There is a tablet which records a bomb falling on the synagogue during Rosh Hashanah services of 1849.

The Tevah was redesigned at the end of the last century. It originally had a large pulpit, surmounted by a crown, which was supported by Corinthian columns. It was flanked by two semicircular stairs. An organ was installed in the last century, but is no longer used during services.

LEVANTINE SYNAGOGUE (Scola)

The Levantine Scola is located across the square from the Spanish Scola. It was built by Middle Eastern Jews between 1538 and 1561. The exterior resembles the Flangini College, which was designed by Baldassarre Longhena. There is a memorial tablet on the front façade which pays tribute to the Jews who died during World War I.

The main entrance to the synagogue is no longer used. The space behind the front doors houses the remains of the Luzzatto Scola, which was located in the Ghetto Nuovo. Several buildings in the Ghetto Nuovo were demolished in 1836. The furnishings from the Luzzatto Scola were then transferred to this location. The vestibule, which is entered via the side entrance of the building, contains two plaques. One refers to "Donations to the Society of Piety and Mercy." The other records the visit of Sir Moses Montefiore in 1875. The main sanctuary is located on the first floor.

The main sanctuary is a large rectangular room, measuring 14 x 9 meters. The Ark and Tevah are placed at opposite ends of the synagogue. The doors of the Ark contain etchings of the Ten Commandments. The Ark is enclosed by a marble, columned baluster. The brass railings were installed in 1786. The Tevah, made of wood, was designed by Andrea Brustolon in the 18th century. It is an exquisite work of art. Two monumental spiral columns rise at the end of the two small lateral semicircular stairs. They join each other at the ceiling, forming an elaborate decorative pattern.

The walls of the synagogue are decorated with Baroque gilding and are covered with red silk damask drapery. The room is illuminated with rich Dutch brass and golden lamps. The women's gallery is enclosed with a grating and conceals the occupants from view. The entire building has recently been restored by the American Committee to Save Venice and by the Community of Venice. This synagogue is used only during the winter season.

The small esplanade in front of the Levantine Scola is called the Corte Scalamatta. The name is derived from the family which lived there. Some say that it is derived from the steep stairs inside the Venetian "skyscrapers," which loom above the street. The Calle del Forno, located on the left of this esplanade, is the site of the matzoh factory.

MIDRASH of LEONE da MODENA

Leone da Modena, also known as Yehuda Aryeh ben Isaac da Modena (1571-1648), was a preacher, apologist, maestro, and author. The "History of Jewish Rites," was one of his many works. His Midrash was located at Calle del Ghetto Vecchio #1222. The Midrash is now closed and abandoned. Directly opposite this Midrash, is the former *Midrash Vivante*, which was founded in 1853.

COMMUNITY OFFICES

The Community Offices are located on the Calle Barucchi (named after the Barukh family). The Renato Maestro Library is also housed in this building. There are 5,400 volumes in the collection. It contains many rare documents dating back to the 1500s. The library was reorganized in 1981 with a contribution from the Region of the Veneto and the Ministry for Cultural and Architectural Goods. It is open to the public on Mondays, Wednesdays, and Fridays, from 8 a.m. to 2 p.m. On Tuesdays and Thursdays, it is open from 1 p.m.

to 7 p.m.

The bridge, Ponte degli Agnudi, was built over the Rio Ghetto in 1541. It leads into the Ghetto Nuovo. This was the first Jewish quarter. It was established in 1516. Seven hundred German and Italian Jews were enclosed within these walls. The ghetto was formed from a trapezoid-shaped field. It was once filled with tall buildings. The life of the community developed within the piazza. All of the shops, banks, etc., faced onto this square.

ITALIAN SYNAGOGUE (Scola)

The synagogue is located on the third floor of the building. There are five large windows facing the piazza. The two memorial plaques near the windows record the destruction of the Temple in Jerusalem and the date when this synagogue was inaugurated (1575).

The interior of the synagogue is similar in plan to the Spanish Scola. The Ark faces the Tevah, which is at the opposite end of the sanctuary. It dates from the early 1500s and was a gift from Beniamino Maria di Consiglio. Four steps lead up to the Ark, which is flanked by four Corinthian columns. The 18th century pulpit is raised by eight steps. It is tucked away in the apse, which is visible from the exterior. The Italian Scola was partially restored by the Jewish Historical Society of Venice and the Italian Committee for Venice. It is not open to the public.

CANTON SYNAGOGUE (Scola)

The Canton Scola was started in 1531 and was enlarged and enriched continually until 1846. The congregation followed the Ashkenazic ritual. The name *Canton* is derived from the name of the family which had constructed the synagogue. Some say that the name is derived from the synagogue's location, on the "corner" of the piazza. Others say that the synagogue was designated to the French Jews in the ghetto, and was called, "*le canton des Juifs.*"

The synagogue is identified by its spherical apse. The five large windows do not face the piazza but rather face the canal. The interior measures 13 x 7 meters. It is of typical Venetian synagogue design. The Ark and Bimah (reading platform) are sumptuously decorated. The Ark is gilded and is designed in late Renaissance style. The sculpted and gilded doors have the Ten Commandments engraved on the exterior. The Ark is surmounted with a crown. The Bimah is gilded and is designed in the 18th century Baroque style. It rests upon five steps

Rialto Bridge of Venice.

Ghetto scene.

Levantine Synagogue.

The Great German Synagogue was built in 1528.

and is located within the apse. Two sets of columns flank its sides.

The walls and ceiling are covered with wood panels, which are decorated with geometric motifs, landscapes and biblical inscriptions. The women's gallery faces the entrance and is screened with a fixed wood grating. The Canton Scola is closed to the public. It is presently being restored by the Venice Committee of St. Louis, Missouri. The Magistrate of Water has already completed work which will stabilize the exterior of the structure.

JEWISH MUSEUM of VENICE

The Jewish Museum is located on the piazza of the Ghetto Nuovo. It is open daily, except on the Sabbath and Jewish holidays. It is open from 10 a.m. to 12 noon, then reopens from 3 p.m. to 5:30 p.m., from March 16 to November 15. Tours of the ghettos depart from this location.

The museum is located on the first floor of the building. It was inaugurated in 1953 and was recently restored and reorganized with a contribution from the Region of Veneto. The museum has displays of sacred furnishings and silver objects, some salvaged from extinct Jewish communities in the Veneto region. There are highly detailed manuscripts from the 15th and 16th centuries.

The Italian Synagogue.

GREAT GERMAN SYNAGOGUE (Scola)

The Great German or Ashkenazic Scola is located on the top floor of the building which houses the Jewish Museum of Venice. This is the oldest synagogue in Venice. It was built by German Jews in 1528. The synagogue was built within an existing room. The furnishings were designed in the standard plan of Venetian synagogues. The Ark and Bimah are placed at opposite ends of the hall. The pews are placed along the long walls and the center of the room remains empty. The hall measures 14 x 7 meters.

The Ark was designed in 1666 and was placed in a niche that was added onto the original structure. It protrudes from the building, above the canal. The Ark rests on four red marble steps. The donor's name, Rabbi Menachem Cividali, is inscribed on the steps. There are four Corinthian columns as well as decorative vases and cornucopia above the Ark. The doors of the Ark are etched with the "Tree of Life" on the exterior and the Ten Commandments, embellished with mother-of-pearl inlay, on the interior. There are two candelabras and two gilded seats, which reproduce the same decorative motifs, on either side of the Ark.

The Bimah is light and simple. It is formed by another niche, which protrudes from the back wall. It is raised on a platform which has similar geometric

Luzzatto Synagogue.

decorations as the ceiling. The trabeation, placed on eight columns, reflects the same motifs as the Ark. The women's gallery protrudes above the hall in an elliptical shape. The walls are covered with red brocaded drapes. This synagogue is no longer used by the community.

A special project is presently being planned by the community. In order to give the tourist an idea of "life in the ghetto," a "model house" would be set up. It would lead from the Jewish Museum into a former living quarter. It would then lead directly into the Canton Scola, go through a lecture hall which would be set up under the synagogue, and continue directly into the Italian Scola. This would be an example of the internal passages which linked the houses and the synagogues, allowing the people to move about the Jewish quarter without ever going outside, and thus avoiding danger.

The Great German Scola has recently been restored by the Historical Society of Venice, the Italian Committee of Venice, and a committee from Frankfurt, Germany.

GHETTO NUOVISSIMO

To the right of the Jewish Museum is a small portal. The Ghetto Nuovissimo is located on the other side of the old wooden bridge. This section was added to the ghetto in 1633. The Ghetto Nuovissimo was inhabited by wealthy Jews. Several of the villas are decorated with ornate moldings and family crests. There were no synagogues or shops in this section of the ghetto. The old "skyscrapers" in the Ghetto Nuovo are clearly visible from this area. At the end of the Calle del Porton, the grooves left by the closure gates are still visible. The portico which leads to the old wooden bridge (on the Ghetto Nuovo side), still contains the hinges of the gates which sealed off the ghetto from the outside world.

One of the three pawn shops which faced the main square in the Ghetto Nuovo was recently found. The name, *banco rosso* (red bank), is visible at #2911. The other two pawn shops were the green and yellow banks, or *banco verde* and *banco giallo.*

JEWISH REST HOME (Casa di Riposo)

The Jewish Rest Home is located on the site of residential buildings which were destroyed during the Napoleonic period. The Rest Home was built at the end of the 19th century. A small chapel is located in the Rest Home. The

Jewish cemetery in the Lido.

furnishings were removed from the Mesullamim Scola, an Ashkenazic synagogue, which was demolished at the end of the 19th century.

It is possible to order a kosher lunch in the Jewish Rest Home. It is necessary to make prior arrangements by calling 716 002.

To the left of the Jewish Rest Home is the morgue. The wall in front of this building contains the Memorial to the Holocaust. There are seven bronze panels designed by Arbit Blatas in 1980. The barbed wires on top of the wall were left after the Nazi occupation.

JEWISH CEMETERIES

The Jewish cemetery is located on the island of Lido. It is along the Riviera San Nicolo. The earliest tombstones date back to 1386. Some of the tombstones are decorated with heraldic motifs. Others have inscriptions in Hebrew, Spanish, and Portuguese, which record the origin of the deceased. Many tombs are sarcophagi, as was common in the 18th century. This ancient cemetery has recently been restored.

The new Jewish cemetery is located on Via Cipro. In 1983, the German community of Neustadt returned the tombstone of Elias Levita, a noted linguist, who was from Neustadt, but died in Venice in 1548.

JEWISH COMMUNITY CENTER

Cannaregio 1118/A Tel. (0141) 715 912

KOSHER RESTAURANT

Beit Chabad *Cannaregio Tel. (41) 716-214*
Gam-Gam *Cannaregio Tel. 715-284*

VERONA

GHETTO SITE Via Portici

The Jews were expelled from Verona in 965. They later were permitted back into the city. In 1146, the commentator and poet Abraham ibn Ezra and Rabbi Eleazar ben Samuel lived in Verona. In the 1300s, the noted poet Shlomo Romans, also known as *Manoello Giudeo,* stayed at the Court of Cangrande della Scala. The Jewish population of Verona in the 1500s was about 400, mostly of German origin. The population later increased with the influx of Jews fleeing the Spanish Inquisition.

Before the Jews were forced into the ghetto, violent arguments and quarrels broke out among the families, about the distribution of houses and apartments. When the Jews were finally forced into the ghetto in 1600, the order was received with great jubilation. This decree forced the Jews to end their bickerings. Every year, since 1700, the Jews of Verona celebrate the date on which they were forced into the ghetto.

The first ghetto was located on Via Portici. In 1655,the Spanish Jews were placed into the Ghetto Nuovo and in the Corte Spagnola. The ghetto gates were torn down in 1797. The Jewish population of Verona was 1,200 in 1861. During the Second World War, 30 Jews were deported. The present population is about 100.

SYNAGOGUE Via Portici #3 Tel. (045) 21112

The imposing synagogue was built in 1864. The seating capacity is over 1,000.

JEWISH CEMETERY Via Antonio Badile (Borgo Venezia)

The first cemeteries are found at Via San Francesco (Campo Fiore) and at

Porta Nuovo. The present cemetery is located at Via Antonio Badile and can be visited on Tuesdays and Thursdays, from 3 to 5 p.m., and on Sundays, from 9 a.m. to 12 noon.

VITTORIO VENETO (Ceneda)

GHETTO SITE Via Lorenzo Da Ponte

ANCIENT SYNAGOGUE Via Lorenzo Da Ponte and Via Manin

In 1637, the Jews were enclosed in a small ghetto. They built a synagogue which followed the Ashkenazic ritual. It was restored and embellished in 1701. It measured 10 x 5.5 x 5.6 meters. The synagogue remained in use until 1910. It was reopened in 1948 for a wedding, but was finally dismantled in the 1950s. Some of the furnishings were sent to Israel. They are now on display in the Israel Museum, in Jerusalem. The remainder of the furnishings were sent to the Jewish Museum in Venice.

JEWISH CEMETERY Cal de Prade

18th century Ark from Vittorio Veneto, now housed in the Israel Museum, Jerusalem.

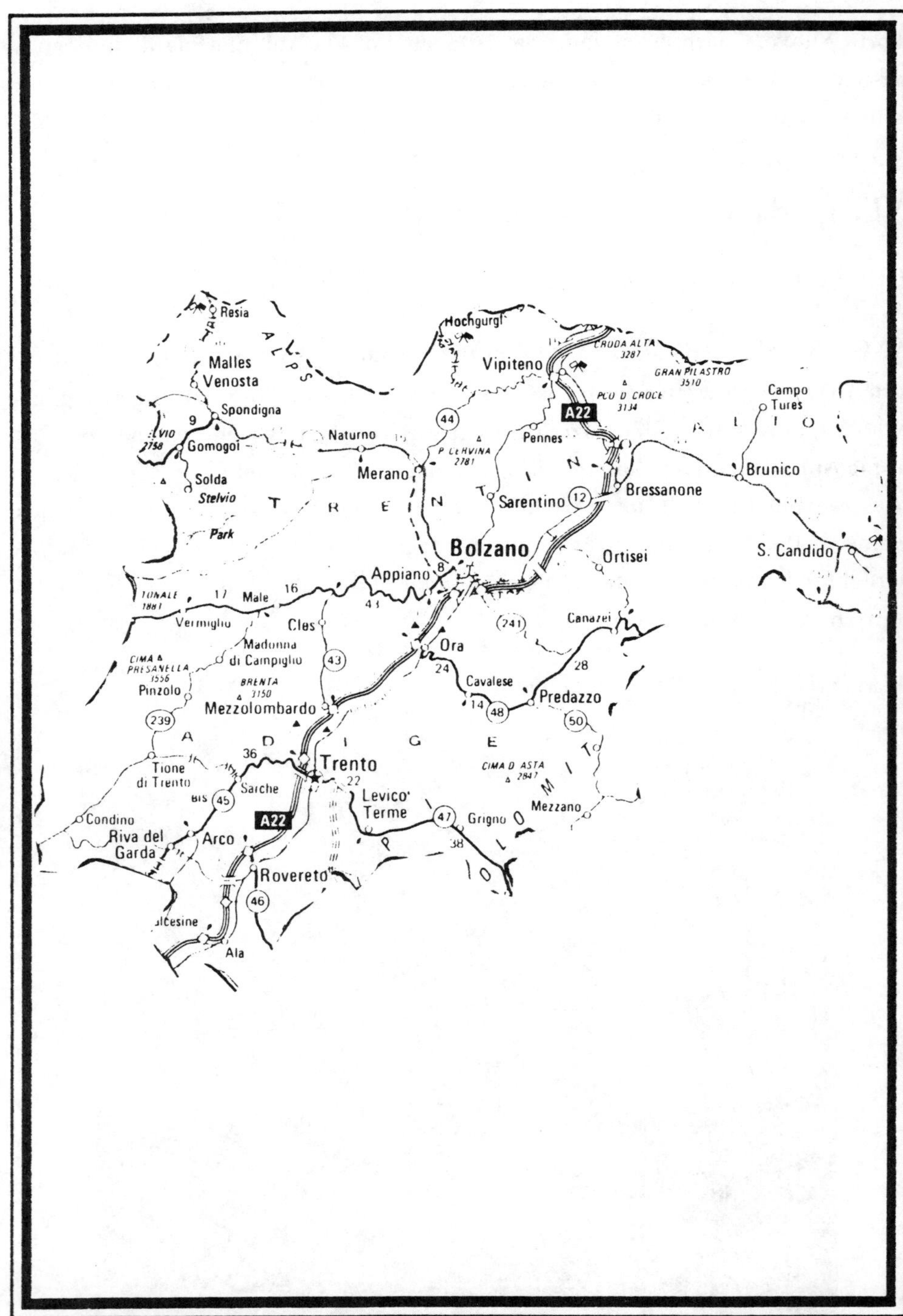

Resia
ALPS
Hochgurgl
Vipiteno
CRODA ALTA
3287
GRAN PILASTRO
3510
PCO D CROCE
3134
A22
Campo
Tures
Malles
Venosta
Spondigna
9
Gomogoi
Naturno
Merano
44
P CERVINA
2781
Pennes
Solda
Stelvio
Park
T R E N T I N
A L T O
Brunico
Sarentino
12
Bressanone
Bolzano
Ortisei
S. Candido
Appiano
TONALE
1881
17
Male
16
Vermiglio
Cles
241
Canazei
Madonna
di Campiglio
43
Ora
CIMA
PRESANELLA
3556
BRENTA
3150
24
Cavalese
28
Pinzolo
Mezzolombardo
14
48
Predazzo
239
50
A D I G E
36
Trento
CIMA D ASTA
2847
Tione
di Trento
Sarche
22
Levico
Terme
Mezzano
45
A22
47
Grigno
Condino
Riva del
Garda
Arco
38
Rovereto
46
Ala

Trentino Alto Adige Region

During the 1300s, Jews lived in this region. They were permitted to operate pawn shops and sometimes charged as much as 86.66 percent interest on loans. This was the going interest rate in the German territories, since liquidity was scarce and it was difficult to open a line of credit.

In the 1400s, the Jews of Trent lived near the Buonconsiglio Castle, along Via Manci. In 1475, Bernard of Feltre accused the Jews of ritual murder. On March 24, the body of a two-year-old child, Simon Underdorben, was discovered in a river. It was discovered on Easter morning. The Jews were accused of killing the child and using his blood to make matzohs for Passover. Eight Jews were immediately arrested and subjected to an inquisition. After seventeen days of torture, one of the accused, an eighty-year-old man, confessed to the crime which he never committed. The accused were executed, even though the Doge of Venice and Pope Sistus IV intervened on behalf of the Jews.

Nevertheless, the local mobs were uncontrollable. In early 1476, another five Jews were killed. The Jews were finally driven out of the City of Trent. This was both to pacify the mobs and for the Jews' own protection. The Cult of Simon became popular throughout the region. In 1852, Gregory XIII included Saint Simon in the Roman Martyrology. March 24, became the "Feast of Saint Simon."

The Jews placed a *chayrem* (excommunication) on the entire region. Jews were never permitted to live in the city or its territory. The prohibition was removed in 1965, when the Sacred Congregation of Rites eliminated the Cult of Simon.

The cities of Bolzano and Merano are located near the Austrian border. The Jews had strong ties with Austrian and central European Jewish communities.

MERANO

Merano has been a popular health resort for those suffering from tuberculosis. Franz Kafka, Sigmund Freud, and Chaim Weizman stayed in this resort. The Jewish national poet, Peretz Smolenskin, was born in Merano. Before the Second World War, the Jewish population was more than 6,000. This was primarily a refugee population. The Jewish population today is about fifty.

SYNAGOGUE Via Schiller #14 Tel. (0473) 34999

The synagogue was built in 1901. It was restored in 1985. The stained-glass windows, designed by Adele Friedenthal, depict various religious symbols and Jewish holidays. The Anne Frank Cultural Center is housed in the same building.

JEWISH CEMETERY Via San Giuseppe

The former cemetery was located on Via San Giocomo #7.

RIVA del GARDA

ANCIENT JEWISH QUARTER

The City of Riva was famous for its Jewish printing house. It was run by Rabbi Giaccobbe Marcaria, who published works in both Hebrew and Latin. The "Book of Rav Alfass" is on display in the Civic Museum of Riva.

The Jews lived in the area of today's City Hall, along Vias Fiume, Diaz, Florida, and Maffei, and along the Vicolos del Ferro, del Fabbro, and della Lucertola. There is an ancient Jewish tombstone embedded in the walls of the City Hall, the Palazzo Pretorio.

TRENT (Trento)

PALAZZO SALVATORI Via Manci

It is believed that the Palazzo Salvatori, on Via Manci, once housed the synagogue. There are two marble entablatures on the façade of this building. One portrays Saint Simon. The other portrays his martyrdom. The home of Simon is located at the Palazzo Bertolazzi, on Via San Simonino. The instruments, which supposedly were used for the ritual murder, were kept in a chapel in the Church of San Pietro.

There are several churches in the Alpine regions of northern Italy which contain frescos devoted to the Cult of Saint Simon. They are located in the Church of Santa Maria in Silvi (in the town of Pisogne); in the Church dell 'Anunciata (in the town of Bienno); in the Parish of Cerveno; and in the churches in Malegno and Niardo.

Ritual murder of Saint Simon in Trent.

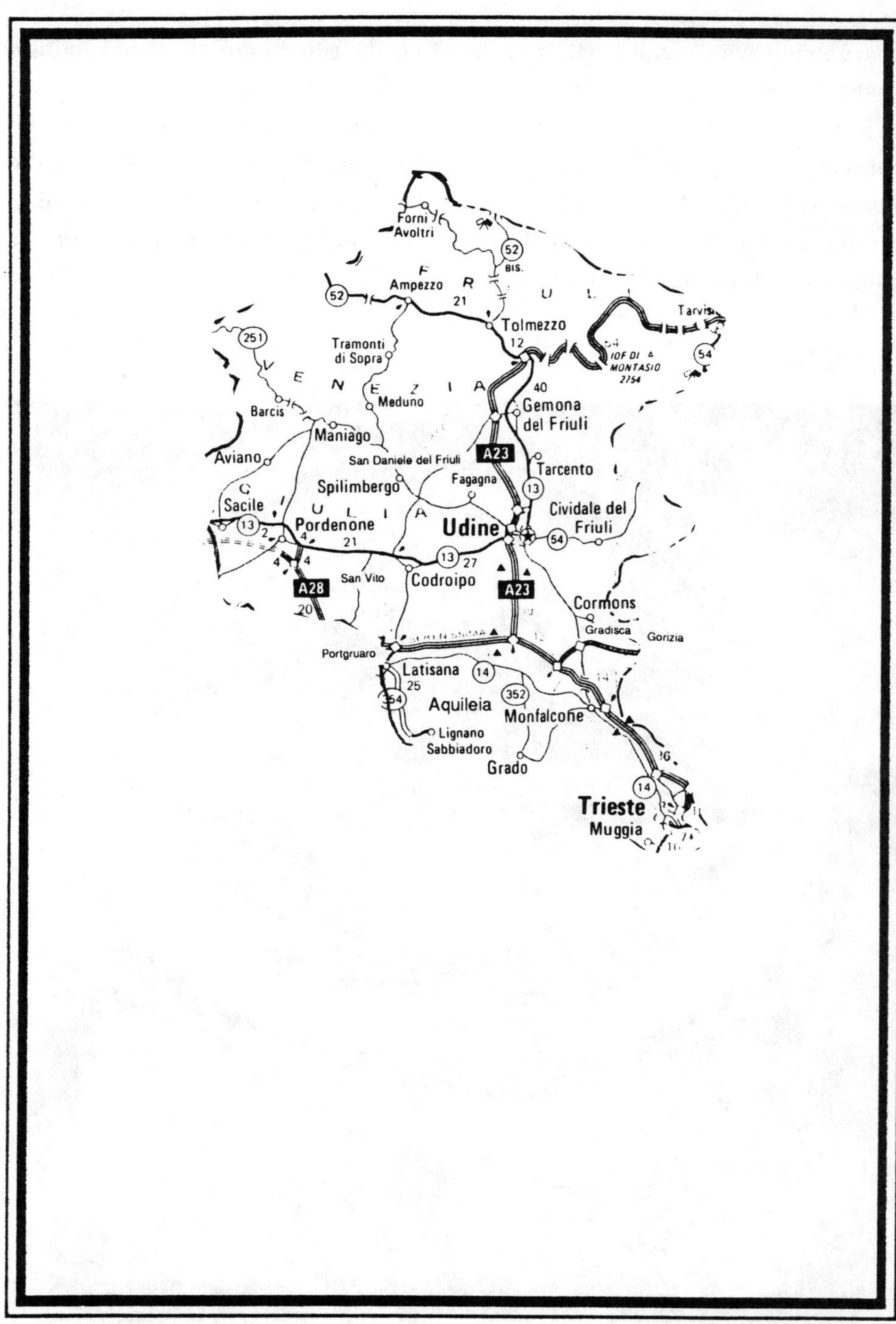

Forni Avoltri
52 BIS.
Ampezzo
Tolmezzo
Tramonti di Sopra
V E N E Z I A
F R I U L I
G I U L I A
Meduno
Barcis
Maniago
Aviano
Gemona del Friuli
A23
Tarcento
San Daniele del Friuli
Fagagna
Spilimbergo
Sacile
Pordenone
Udine
Cividale del Friuli
San Vito
Codroipo
A28
Cormons
Gradisca
Gorizia
Portgruaro
Latisana
Aquileia
Monfalcone
Lignano Sabbiadoro
Grado
Trieste
Muggia
MONTASIO 2754
Tarvisio

Friuli Venezia Giulia Region

The present region unites two geographic areas. The areas east of Isonzo were under the Austrian rule, while the areas west of Isonzo were ruled by the Venetian Republic. In 1450, Francesca Sforza drove out the Tuscan moneylenders. The Jews prospered since they were the exclusive moneylenders in the region. This changed in the 1600s, when the Christian-run *Monte di Pieta* pawn shops were created. The Jews abandoned moneylending and went into other trades. Some went into tailoring, while others went into a new industry, silk weaving.

In Spilimbergo, the Jews were permitted to continue living in their own own quarters, instead of being forced into a ghetto. The only restriction was that they were "ghettoized." The sound of the "Ave Maria" marked the start of the evening curfew. Jews had to remain in their homes until dawn.

Some Jewish communities such as San Tomasco di Collorado, Maniago, Plasencis, and Rivignano completely disappeared. Others, such as Trieste, Gorizia, and Istria prospered and flourished.

AQUILEIA

ANCIENT SYNAGOGUE

Archaeologists claim that the Monastery of Aquileia was originally a 4th century synagogue.

CIVIDALE del FRIULI

ARCHAEOLOGICAL MUSEUM

There are 16 Jewish tombstones which were excavated from a former cemetery. The oldest stone, dated 1342, tells of a woman who died in prison, after having been severely tortured for defending her Jewish faith. Avigdor Cividal, the noted Talmudic scholar and rabbi of Venice in 1597, was born in Cividale del Friuli.

GORIZIA

GHETTO SITE Via Graziadio Isaia Ascoli

The ghetto was established in Gorizia in 1698. It was located on Via Graziadio Isaia Ascoli, near the Church of San Giovanni. The Jews were permitted to purchase their homes, instead of renting them, as was the common practice. In 1850, there were 314 Jews living in the city. Today, there are no Jews in Gorizia.

ISAIA ASCOLI RESIDENCE Via Ascoli #1

Isaia Ascoli was a noted philologist in the 19th century. His home has been turned into a national landmark. The young poet and philosopher Carlo Michelstaedter was a member of the Ascoli family.

ANCIENT SYNAGOGUE Via Ascoli

The synagogue was built in 1699 and contained several congregations "superimposed" within the one structure. It was organized as a German congregation. A small Polish chapel was located on the ground floor. The entire structure has been restored. Inquire at the City Hall for information about visiting the ancient synagogue. The building is now used for conferences and cultural events. The synagogue is used only on special occasions. The building resembles a typical country villa rather than a house of worship. The synagogue was saved from destruction during a war in 1761. In honor of that event, the ancient congregation celebrated a special *Purim* of thanks.

JEWISH CEMETERY

The Jewish cemetery of Valdirose is located in Nova Gorica, in the Yugoslavian section of the city. The cemetery dates back to 1371. It was used until the1800s.

GRADISCA

GHETTO SITE Via Petrarca

The Jews were forced into the ghetto in 1768 but only lived there until 1782. The houses were numbered with Roman numerals.

ANCIENT SYNAGOGUE Via Petrarca #IV

JEWISH CEMETERY Via del Campi #15

SAN DANIELE del FRIULI

ANCIENT SYNAGOGUE Piazzetta Cattaneo

The ancient synagogue, dating back to the 17th century, was located behind the Duomo, in Piazzetta Cattaneo. The furnishings were shipped to Israel in the 1950s. They have been incorporated into the Italian Synagogue in Jerusalem.

JEWISH CEMETERY

The cemetery was created in 1735 and is located on the shore of Lake Muris, in the area of Comugne.

SAN VITO & PORTOGRUARO

JEWISH CEMETERY Borgo San Francesco

There is an inverted Jewish tombstone attached to the Agricultural Storage House in Savorgnano, a section in San Vito. The tombstone belongs to Shmuel ben Yehudah Romanin, who was a noted physician in Padua. He died in 1798. The Romanin house was located on the Contrada di Codamala.

17th century Ark from San Daniele del Fiuli, now in the Italian Synagogue, Jerusalem.

SPILIMBERGO

ANCIENT SYNAGOGUE Piazza San Rocco

The Jews in this city were not required to move to a ghetto, but were rather "ghettoized" in their homes. The former synagogue was located in the Saraval Building, on the Piazza San Rocco (near the Palazzo Griz). The synagogue burned down in 1917.

TRIESTE

There was a small Jewish settlement in Trieste in the 11th century. It was not until the 14th century, when the city was annexed by Austria, that Jews were involved in banking and trading. Over the centuries, German, Spanish, French, and Levantine Jews poured into Trieste.

Austria protected the Jews of the city and granted them civil rights. In 1693, however, the Jews were forced into a ghetto. The first ghetto was on Corte Trauner, in Crosada. The second ghetto was situated in the Riborgo quarter, near Borsa.

In 1771, Empress Maria Theresa issued the "Imperial Laws of Tolerance." The Jews were given the right to openly profess their religion. Forced baptisms were prohibited. The Jews were permitted to open industries and commercial companies. In 1782, Giuseppe II opened all professions to the Jews. The Jews were now permitted to rent land. If they wished to own land, they had to convert to Christianity. Jewish schools were established. The ghetto was officially dismantled in 1785.

Jews founded banks and insurance companies. Many of the more influential Jews were granted titles of nobility by the Viennese Court: the Morpurgos, the Parentes, the Vivantes became barons, the Eisners of Eisenhoff, the Hierschels, the Morpurgos of Nilma, the De Daninos, the Frigessis of Rattalma, and the Richettis of Terralba became Knights of the Empire. In 1861, there were seven Jewish city counselors. Sir Raffaele Luzzatto and Baron Giuseppe Morpurgo were elected Deputies to the Vienna Parliament.

This integration into society ultimately led the Jewish community away from traditional Orthodox ways of life. Trieste was a veritable melting pot of central European culture. It reproduced the life-style of Jews in Vienna. Jews assimilated into the society and went into the liberal and intellectual professions. Psychoanalysis found its first application and study through the works of Edoardo Weiss (1899-1970) and Ettore Schmitz, also known as "Italo Svevo." Some of the noted poets, writers, and editors include Umberto Saba, Roberto Bazlan, and Giacomo de Benedetti.

GHETTO SITE

The first ghetto was located on Corte Trauner, Via dei Capitelli dell 'Arco di Riccardo, in Piazza San Silvestro. The ghetto was instituted in 1693. The building with Gothic windows on the upper floor, on Via Trauner, is believed to have been a synagogue.

The second ghetto was located in the Riborgo section, near the Borsa. The Jews were assigned thirteen houses. The perimeter was enclosed by Contrada Riborgo, Contrada Malcanton, and the long Contrada Beccherie. One of the gate hooks is still visible at Via Beccherie #3. There is a sign indicating that this street was once the butcher's quarter. The sign reads "Rubenstein carni (meats)." The ghetto was officially dismantled in 1785.

ANCIENT SYNAGOGUES

There were three synagogues in the ghetto. The first, known as the Scola Piccola, was located at Via Beccherie and Contrada delle Scuole. It was built by German Jews in 1748. It was last used by Jews from Corfu, Greece, in 1935. The synagogue furnishings were sent to a synagogue in Tel Aviv (Rechov Smuts) in 1956. The Academy of Buona Dottrina, also known as the Midrash Lekach Tov, was established in 1802 by Rabbi Isaiah Norsa. It was located in the Scola Piccola.

The second synagogue was located in the Piazzetta delle Scuole ebraiche. It was built in 1798 by architect Bolzani and followed the Ashkenazic ritual. In 1934, the synagogue was destroyed by fire. The Ark was sent to Fiume. The third synagogue in the ghetto followed the Sephardic ritual. It was located on the site of today's Police Headquarters. The synagogue was demolished in 1928. Its Ark was sent to Abbazia. There was a fourth synagogue, but it was located outside the ghetto, on Via del Monte. It was built in 1805 and was known as the Scola Vivante. It was the most lavish synagogue in Trieste, but has been demolished.

SYNAGOGUE Via San Francesca #19 Tel. (040) 768 171

The Jewish community wanted to build a synagogue which would display the

Great Synagogue of Trieste.

Old ghetto scene, Trieste.

18th century marble Ark from Trieste, shipped to the Central Synagogue Rassco-Tzafon in Tel Aviv, Israel.

prosperity which it had achieved. The architects Ruggero and Arduino Berlam were commissioned. They had an unlimited budget. In 1912, the synagogue was consecrated, with the presence of Prince Hohenlohe.

The monumental structure is designed with Romanesque and Classical elements. There are exquisite floral designs etched into the Istrian limestone façades. Above one of the doors are symbols of the Jewish community; a crown and the breastplate of Aaron (the priest), the palms, and the sheaf of corn.

The main sanctuary is rectangular in shape. There are three aisles that end at the large apse. The Ark and Bimah are located within the apse. The apsidal vault has gold mosaics and is adorned with grape-leaf and floral friezes. The walls of the apse are covered with dark green marble. The imposing organ, decorated with Stars of David, is situated in the women's gallery. The women's gallery is used only on major holidays. Other times, a section in the men's section is reserved for the women. The main sanctuary is used only for Sabbath and holiday services. The congregation follows the Ashkenazic ritual. The small chapel is used on Mondays, Thursdays, Rosh Chodesh (new moon), and on minor holidays. It follows the Sephardic ritual. There is a mikveh, which has recently been restored, in the basement of the building.

The Community Center houses the offices of the rabbi, the Emilio Screiber Library, and the historical archives. The "Patenti" of Maria Theresa, which granted protection to the Jews of Trieste, is housed in these archives. There is a memorial plaque in honor of Sir Moses Montefiore.

RISIERA di SAN SABA (Detention Camp) Largo Martiri della Risiera

The ghetto and the four synagogues were dismantled during the rule of the Fascists. In the 1940s, many Jews left the city. The community was reduced from 6,000 to 2,300. On July 18, 1942, the Fascists destroyed the main synagogue of Trieste. Between 1943 and 1944, 837 Jews were arrested and sent to the Risiera di San Saba. There were many prison cells and torture rooms. The only crematorium in Italy was housed in this complex. The Jews were later deported to concentration camps in Germany.

The Risiera di San Saba is now a national memorial. It can be visited daily (except Monday), from 9 a.m. to 1 p.m.

JEWISH CEMETERY Via della Pace #4

The first Jewish cemetery was located on the Via del Monte. It was closed during the mid-1800s. Thereafter, the Jews buried their dead in the cemetery of

Santa Anna. The original cemetery was transformed into a "Remembrance Park" in 1909.

PORT of TRIESTE

Between 1820 and 1918, four million Jews departed from the Port of Trieste for the United States, South America, and Palestine. In 1921, in order to assist Jews who wished to go to Palestine, the Italian Committee for the Assistance of Emigrants was established. The old-timers in Trieste recall how, at the departure of the ships "Jerusalem" and "Galilee," the dock-workers sang the *Hatikvah,* the Jewish National Anthem, in Triestine dialect. In 1933, when refugees from Hitler's Germany arrived at Trieste, they were bound for Palestine and designated the port as the "Port of Zion."

JEWISH REST HOME Via Cologna #29 Tel. 568 578

Kosher meals are available, by prior arrangement only.

UDINE

ANCIENT SYNAGOGUE Via Manin

The former Ashkenazic Synagogue was located on the first floor of a private home on Via Manin. It was built in 1840. It had exquisite frescos painted on its walls. It was last used by Jewish soldiers who celebrated *Shavuot,* during World War I. Today, there is only one Jewish family left in the city.

There was a small chapel on Via R. Battastig. It existed in the 1920s-30s and used the Torahs from the City of San Daniele. Notable citizens such as the Baron and Senator Elia Morpurgo, were deported during the Nazi invasion.

JEWISH CEMETERY

The first cemetery was located in Riva d'Isola, on Calle Agricola, near Via Liruti #18. It dates back to 1045. It was used until the 19th century. The present cemetery is located in the cemetery of San Vitale.

Jews await ship to Palestine in the port of Trieste.

Risiera di San Saba detention camp.

Monticelli D'Ongina
Piacenza
Nibbiano
Rivergaro
Busseto
Soragna
Bobbio
Bettola
Fidenza
Ferriere
Salsomaggiore
Terme
Ottone
Bore
Bardi
Varsi
Parma
Fornovo
di Taro
Bedonia
APPENNINO
Guastalla
Correggio
Reggio
Nell'Emilia
Carpi
Mirandola
Bondeno
Cento
Ferrara
Copparo
Formignana
Castelnova
ne' Monti
Scandiano
Modena
S. Giovanni
in Persiceto
Codigoro
Carpineti
Sassuolo
Vignola
Bazzano
Bologna
Molinella
Portomaggiore
Pavullo nel
Frignano
Oliveto
Argenta
Comacchio
Zocca
Sasso
Marconi
Vergato
Pianoro
Alfonsine
Castelnuovo di
Garfagnana
Abetone
EMILIANO
Imola
Lugo
Marina di
Ravenna
Ravenna
Castiglione
dei Pepoli
Faenza
Forlì
Bertinoro
Cesenatico
Rocca
S. Casciano
Cesena
Borello
S. Piero
in Bagno
Rimini
Riccione
A1
A15
A22
A13
A14
A16

Emilia Romagna Region

This region was once divided into three political divisions: the Parmese States of Parma and Piacenza; the Estensi States of Modena, Reggio Emilia, and Ferrara; and the territories of the Papal States of Bologna, Romagna, and Ferrara (after 1598).

The first Jews settled in the Parmese States in the beginning of the 15th century. They originated from Germany and southern Italy. They were permitted to open banks and lending institutions. In 1488, the Christian-run *Monte di Pieta* pawn shops were opened and the Jews were forced to leave the cities of Parma and Piacenza. They settled in the small communities of Fidenza, Busseto, Colorno, Roccabianca, San Secondo, Sissa, Soragna, and Torrechiara, in the Province of Parma. They established other communities in Borgovono, Cortemaggiore, Fiorenzuola d'Arda, Guardamiglio, Monticelli d'Ongina, Rivaltoa San Giovanni, and Vigoleno, in the Province of Piacenza.

In the early 1900s, the Jews left the small agricultural communities and settled in the large cities of Parma and Soragna. All that remains of the former Jewish settlements are the old cemeteries.

The Estes family implanted a policy of tolerance and patronage throughout the Estensi States. The Jews of Modena and Reggio Emilia enjoyed greater liberties, even though they were enclosed in ghettos. When Ferrara was annexed by the Papal States in 1598, many Jews left.

Since the 1200s, the countryside in this province was studded with small pockets of Jewish life. In 1767, the *Monte di Pieta* caused many of the small Jewish communities such as Mirandola, Formiggine, Brescello, Luzzara, and Sassuolo to vanish. The Jews who lived in Scandiano, Carpi, Novellara, Corregio, and Finale Emilia were occupied in the silk industry.

There were Jewish communities in the Papal State of Romagna in the 15th and 16th centuries. The Jews of Rimini, Forli, Faenz, Ravenna, Russi, Cesena, and Bertinoro were involved in the maritime trade as early as the 13th century. There was a house identified as the "House of Ovadia," in Bertinoro, which was an important Rabbinical Academy.

In 1555, the Jews were forced to leave these cities. Some moved into the ghettos of Ferrara, Cento, and Lugo. Others left the province of the Papal States. The Jewish community of Ravenna disappeared. All that remains is the Jewish cemetery in the nearby town of Piangipane.

During the summer season, several hotels in the region offer kosher facilities. For information, call the the Jewish Communal Office in Ferrara at (0532) 47004 or 47539.

Medieval Jewish wedding.

BERTINORO

HOUSE of OVADIA

Ovadia ben Avraham di Bertinoro (1450-1516), the celebrated commentator of the Mishnah, lived in this house. It is located in the old Jewish quarter of the city. His works were printed in Venice in 1548 and were known for their clear and precise interpretations of the Mishnah. The front façade of the house contains a triangular emblem portraying a lamp.

BOLOGNA

Jews have lived in Bologna as far back as the 3rd and 4th centuries. The Jewish community was characterized by continuous expulsions, returns, enclosures in the ghetto, and emancipation. The first ghetto was instituted in 1366. A second ghetto was established in 1566. In 1593, the Jews were expelled from Bologna. In 1859, the Jews finally gained equal rights. Before that date, Bologna was under the jurisdiction of the Papal State. They were subjected to forced sermons and baptisms. In 1858, a six-year-old Jewish child, Edgardo Mortara, was kidnaped by missionaries. They brought the child to Rome, where he was placed in a Catholic school. He later joined the Augustine Order, and never returned to his faith.

After 1859, Jews dedicated themselves to the liberal professions, which were once prohibited. Some went into journalism. Emilio Zamorani founded the city newspaper,"Il Resto del Carlino." It is still being published.

The *Delasem,* which stood for the Delegation for the Assistance of Emigrants, was headed by Mario Finzi during the war years. In March, 1944, Finzi was arrested, brought to the detention camp in Fossoli, and ultimately deported to Auschwitz. In the winter of 1943, 83 Jews were deported. The leader of the Jewish community, Rabbi Alberto Orvieto, was among the deported.

Today, there are approximately 230 Jews living in Bologna. This is excluding the several hundred Jewish students who attend the University.

GHETTO SITE

The ghetto doors were located at Piazza Ravegnana and Via dei Guidei and at Via del Carro and Via Zamboni. The "red light" district of Bologna was located at Vicolo Tubertini and Via Oberdan. The Jews were forced to move into this section. The Hotel of the Red Hat (Albergo Al Cappello Rosso) is located at Via de 'Fusari #9. This was once the only hotel which permitted Jewish travelers to stay as guests. The Jews, at that time, were required to wear a red hat which distinguished them from the general public. Today, the glass doors of the hotel portray the red hats worn by the cardinals.

The Literary Academy was established in 1545 by Achille Bocchi. It was located at Via Goita #18. There are two inscriptions along the front façade of the building. One inscription is a verse from Horace and is written in Latin. The other inscription is taken from the Psalms and is written in Hebrew. The inscriptions warn the scholars, "Do not use the Academy for your lies or personal quarrels."

SYNAGOGUE Via de 'Gombruti #9 Tel. (051) 232 066

The first synagogue on this site occupies the front portion of the complex. It was organized in 1829 by Angelo Carpi, who came from Cento. The small chapel is located on the ground floor. The first floor contains the offices of the Jewish community, the rabbi's apartment, a small elementary Hebrew school (no longer in use), and a kosher cafeteria. One of the few remaining red brick towers in the city is located above this building. There is a mikveh in the cellar.

The main sanctuary was built in the second wing of this complex. It was designed by architect Attilio Muggia in 1928. This portion of the complex was bombed in 1943. It was rebuilt in 1954 by the son of the architect, Guido Muggia.

JEWISH CEMETERY Via della Certosa #18

The first cemetery was located outside of Porta San Stefano. In 1593, the Jews took their dead with them when they were expelled from the city. The present cemetery is located at Via della Certosa and was established in 1800.

CIVIC MUSEUM Portici del Pavaglione #2

There are several ancient Jewish tombstones dating back to the 1500s on display in the Civic Museum. There are several rare manuscripts and books in the University Library, located at Via Zamboni #35.

Komemiyut Synagogue in Jerusalem houses the 1727 Ark from Busseto.

BUSSETO

ANCIENT SYNAGOGUE Via Ferro #13

The furnishings from this Ashkenazic congregation were sent to Israel in 1966. They are now incorporated into the Komemiyut Synagogue, on Chovevay

Zion Street, in Jerusalem. This is the same street on which Martin Buber lived.

Busseto is the home of Giuseppe Verdi. In 1831, a gifted Jewish businessman, Isacco Levi, was murdered in Busseto. The episode made such an impression on Antonio Barezzi, a Jewish landowner, that he searched for a young man who would live in his villa, and if the necessity arose, defend the villa and its inhabitants. Giuseppe Verdi, then 18 years old, was selected for this task. Barezzi became Verdi's patron, and later, his father-in-law.

JEWISH CEMETERY Via Bersano

The Jewish cemetery can be visited by contacting the Muggia family at Via Provesi #36 or call (0524) 92222. The Jewish artist, Isacco Giocchino Levi (1818-1909), is buried in this cemetery. His paintings are on display in the Civic Museum, in the Palazzo Pallavicino, the Verdi Theater, and in the halls of the local *Monte di Pieta.*

The Muggia family has produced a special dessert called *Spongata* in its small bakery since 1867. According to some scholars, it was introduced to Italy by the Spanish Jews in the 15th century. The ingredients are as follows: flower, butter, sugar, eggs, milk, and lemon rind, which make the dough; it is then filled with honey, marmalade, candied fruit, almonds, and pine seeds. The dessert is then dusted with toasted bread crumbs and sprinkled with spices. It can be purchased directly from the Muggia bakery in Busseto. This torte has become a speciality of Emilian cuisine.

CARPI

ANCIENT SYNAGOGUE Via G. Rovighi #57

This synagogue was closed in 1922. The frescos on the interior walls were designed by the Modenese artists, Venturi and Manzini. Some of the furnishings were sent to the synagogue in Modena. Other parts of the furnishings were sent to the synagogue in the Ayanot Agricultural School, in Israel.

JEWISH CEMETERY Via del Cimitero Israelitico

FOSSOLI PRISON CAMP

In 1942, the Fossoli Prison Camp was built in the suburb of Carpi. It was initially designed for the prisoners of the Allied Forces. In 1943, it was taken over by the Nazis, who transformed it into a detention camp for political and racial prisoners. The trains, filled with Jewish prisoners, departed for the German death camps from Fossoli. The Nazis abandoned the camp after the Allies and partisans were advancing, in 1944. The prisoners, however, were transferred to the prison camp in Bolzano.

The empty barracks were later used by the religious community of Nomadelfia. Under the guidance of Zeno Saltini, the former camp was spiritually and symbolically redeemed. It became the Village of San Marco and housed Istrian refugees until the 1960s. Since then, the barracks have been abandoned.

The Museum of the Political and Racial Deportees in the Nazi Extermination Camps has been established in a wing of the old Pio Castle. It is located on Piazza dei Martiri. It was designed by architects Begiojoso, Peressutti, and Rogers, with the assistance of artist Renato Guttoso.

The museum consists of fourteen halls which contain works by Picasso, Longoni, Guttoso, Cagli, and Léger. Letters written by partisans who were condemned to death, are inscribed on the walls. There are glass-encased documents and mementos. Exhibit Hall #13 contains the names of the deportees inscribed on its vaults. The exterior of the building has a sculpture consisting of fifteen stars. This is symbolic of the fifteen Nazi concentration camps which existed throughout Europe during the war.

Fossoli prison camp.

18th century Ark from Cento, now in the Givat Meir Synagogue at Natania, Israel.

CENTO

GHETTO SITE Via Provenzal

When the ghetto was dismantled in 1797, the three doors of the ghetto were torn down and burned. In 1815, the "Restoration" period reinstituted the ghetto. The doors were replaced, at the expense of the Jews. The ghetto was dismantled, for a second time, in 1831. The doors, however, were not destroyed but rather, were kept in storage in a nearby barn. They were finally burned thirty years later, when Cento was annexed by the Kingdom of Italy.

ANCIENT SYNAGOGUE Via Provenzal #3

This synagogue was in use until the 1930s. All of the furnishings have been removed to the synagogue in Ferrara. The plaque on the wall of the former synagogue memorializes the English Prime Minister, Benjamin Disraeli (1804-1881), whose paternal grandfather had left Cento for Great Britain in 1748. Rabbi Graziadio Neppi participated in the Napoleonic "Sanhedrin" in 1806.

JEWISH CEMETERY Via degli Israeliti #1

This cemetery is located in Pieve de Cento. For information about visiting this cemetery, call (051) 905389.

CORREGIO

ANCIENT GHETTO Via Casati

The 18th century Ark was sent to the Hapoel Hamizrachi Synagogue in Jerusalem.

CORTEMAGGIORE

ANCIENT SYNAGOGUE Via Cavour & Via IV Novembre

The Ark of this former synagogue is now on display in the Jewish Museum in Soragna. The doors of the Ark were sent to Israel.

JEWISH CEMETERY Via del Morlenzo

The last Jew in Cortemaggiore, Oreste Muggia, died in 1984, at the age of 105.

FERRARA

There were Jews living in Ferrara as early as the 13th century. The community prospered throughout the 15th century. This was primarily due to the Este Dukes, who explicitly declared themselves the "protectors of the Jews." In 1451, they refused to expel the Jews as per instructions of the Pope.

The city welcomed Jewish refugees from Spain in 1492, from Germany in 1530, from the Duchy of Milan in 1540, and from the Papal State of Bologna in

The Cortemaggiore synagogue furnishings were sent to the Jewish Museum in Soragna.

1569. The Jewish population was 2,000. There were ten synagogues and many Jewish printing houses. The "Bible of Ferrara" was printed in 1553.

In 1598, the principal sovereign of the Este family died, without an heir. Ferrara was now ruled by the Papal State. The Este family moved its Court to Modena and was followed by many Jews. The over 1,500 Jews who remained in Ferrara were subjected to new and harsh rules. They had to wear the identification mark, were not permitted to purchase land, were forced to close seven of their ten synagogues, and , in 1627, were forced to live in a ghetto. The ghetto lasted for over a century.

At the beginning of the 20th century, there were 1,300 Jews living in Ferrara. Renzo Ravenna was the mayor between the war years. In 1938, the Fascists imposed their harsh rules. Children had to leave the public schools and the adults were forced out of their jobs. Giorgio Bassani recorded these events very effectively in his book "The Garden of Finzi Contini."

On the evening of Rosh Hashanah, September 21, 1941, the first devastation of the synagogue occurred. The local Fascists desecrated the synagogue and rounded up hundreds of Jews. Two hundred Jews were deported by the Nazis. Only five returned. Today, there are about 100 Jews living in Ferrara.

GHETTO SITE Via Mazzini

The Jews were forced into the ghetto in 1627. It was enclosed by five gates. They were located at the rear of the Piazza Trento e Trieste, at Via Mazzini, at Via Vignatagliata, at Via Vittorio, opposite Piazza Lampronti, at Via delle Scienze, and at Via dei Contrari.

The commercial section of the ghetto was located at the entrance to Via Mazzini. Before the last war, Nuta Ascoli, a local grocer, was famous for his Ferrarese kosher "buricche" and sturgeon caviar, from the Po River.

There are two memorial tablets at Via Vignatagliata #33, which record the home of Isacca Lampronti, the noted rabbi, doctor, and philosopher. He was the author of *Pachad Yitzchok*, the best known and most popular Talmudic encyclopedia.

Via Vignatagliata #79 was the location of the school used during the Racial Laws under Fascist rule. It housed students from kindergarten through high school. Giorgio Bassani was a teacher in this school.

ANCIENT SYNAGOGUE Via Vittorio #39

This was the site of the Spanish Synagogue. The backs of the houses on Via Mazzini were facing outside of the ghetto. It was forbidden to have any opening which looked outside the ghetto. Some of those bricked-up windows are still visible.

SYNAGOGUE Via Mazzini #95 Tel. (0532) 47004

This building houses the Jewish Community Center, the rabbi's apartment, and two synagogues. The Scola Fanese contains furnishings which were removed from the synagogue in Cento. This chapel is used daily. The main sanctuary is located in the other wing of the complex, just beyond the courtyard. There is a memorial plaque dedicated to Sir Samuele Melli, the benefactor who donated the land upon which the synagogue was built, in 1481.

The large Scola Tedesca is used only on major Jewish holidays. A long corridor leads to the room which housed the Scola Italiana or Italian ritual synagogue. It contains three Arks which date from the 18th century. They were restored in

Ferrara Synagogue.

1957.

JEWISH CEMETERY Via delle Vigne #2

The first cemetery was located near the Church of San Gerolamo. After 1200, it was moved to the Contrada Santa Maria Nuovo, near the Church of San Giustina. In 1626, the present Jewish cemetery, at Via Delle Vigne #2, was opened along the old walls of the city.

FINALE EMILIA

GHETTO SITE Via Morandi

ANCIENT SYNAGOGUE Via Morandi #12

Note: The Kiosk Bar, located in the Piazza de Giordini, serves a "Torta degli ebrei" (Torte of the Jews). It is available during the winter holiday season in the pastry shop. It is a salted pizza made with a bread dough, lard, and melted Parmesan cheese. (This product is not kosher.)

FIORENZUOLA d'ARDA

ANCIENT SYNAGOGUE Via Garibaldi #52

The synagogue building was sold in the 1970s. The Ark and the Tevah were sent to the Scola Shapira, in Milan. Some of the other furnishings were sent to the Jewish Museum in Soragna.

LUGO di ROMAGNA

GHETTO SITE Corso Matteotti

The Jewish community was established in the 1200s. It reached its maximum religious and cultural importance in the 16th century, with the Rabbis Samuel del Vecchio and Beniamino Raffaele de Arezzo. The first ghetto was instituted in 1639 and was located in the Codalunga area. In 1732, the Jewish population in the ghetto was approximately 4,000. The ghetto was dismantled and reinstituted several times before its final dismantling in 1833. The ghetto doors were replaced with marble columns and were inscribed with the word "ghetto."

Ancient ghetto of Lugo di Romagna.

When Pope Pius IX stopped in Lugo during a Pastoral visit in 1857, the Jews erected a triumphal arch at the entrance to the ghetto. It was inscribed with the words, "To the most lenient Prince." The Jewish community also composed a special hymn, in Hebrew, for this special occasion.

At the end of the 19th century, many Jews left Lugo and moved to larger cities. The community continued to decline, but still maintained its synagogue until 1938. During the war, twenty-six Jews were deported. In 1944, most of the ghetto area, including the two synagogues, were destroyed. The few surviving Torahs are presently housed in the synagogue in Ferrara.

At the end of May or early June, the local Parish celebrates the "Festival of the Ghetto." It coincides with the Jewish holiday of *Shavuot*. The festivities take place on Corso Matteotti.

JEWISH CEMETERY Via di Giu

The Jewish cemetery is located just outside the old ghetto area. It was established in 1877. The tombstones from the earlier cemetery were transferred to this location. The oldest tombstone, of a certain Moshe Mih-ha Pesachim (the Hebrew name of the Castelfranco family from Reggio), dates from 1285. For further information, contact the Marach family at (0545) 27743.

MODENA

The Jewish presence in Modena dates back to 1025. Many Jews were attracted to the city because of the tolerance of the Estensi family in 1598. The Jewish population swelled to over 1,000. In 1638, they were forced into the ghetto. There were three synagogues which followed the Italian, Spanish, and German rituals. There was also a famous School of Judaic and Cabbalistic Studies, which was attended by such prominent scholars as Abramo Graziani, Aaron Berechiach da Modena, Abramo Rovigo, and Israele Cohen.

GHETTO SITE Via Torre and Via Emilia

There were four gates in the ghetto. They were located at Via Torre and Via Emilia; Via Taglio and Via Cesare Battisti; Vicolo Squallore and Via Emilia; and at Via Blasia and Via Emilia. There is a plaque at Via Taglio #2 which memorializes Judge Donato Donati (1880-1946), who belonged to one of the oldest and most important Jewish families in Modena.

SYNAGOGUE Piazza Mazzini #26 Tel. (059) 223 978

The synagogue was built in 1873 and was designed by Ludovico Maglietta. It was decorated by the artist Ferdinando Manzini. The Classical façade has four Corinthian columns. The main sanctuary is used only on major Jewish holidays. The mikveh was located in the basement of the building, but is no longer in operation.

GERMAN SYNAGOGUE Via Cappellini #10

This synagogue conducts daily prayer services. The building contains a matzoh factory. The former German Yeshiva, located on the first floor, is now used as the residence of the rabbi.

ANCIENT SYNAGOGUE Via Cappellini #25

This was the site of the Spanish Synagogue.

JEWISH CEMETERY San Cataldo

The first cemetery was located at Via Verdi and Via Mascagni. The present Jewish cemetery is located adjoining the Catholic cemetery. One section of the partition between the two cemeteries is designed in glass. It separates two soldiers who died together in France, during World War II. One soldier, Pio Donati, was Jewish; the other soldier, Francesco Ferrari, was Catholic.

DELASEM OFFICE Villa Emma

The Delegation for the Assistance of Emigrants, *Delasem*, saved many refugees before and during World War II. The office was located in Villa Emma.

MONTICELLI d'ONGINA

ANCIENT SYNAGOGUE Via Garibaldi #17

JEWISH CEMETERY Via T. Edison #2

The original cemetery was located on Via Repubblica, in Borgonovo di Monticelli. The farmers never cultivated the surrounding lands, even after the cemetery was closed and the tombstones were removed. This was done out of respect for the deceased.

There is a local custom in this town in which a "pasta all 'ebrea" is eaten on solemn Christian holidays.

OLIVETO

HOUSE of the JEW

In the Valley of Samoggia, there are ruins of a large 15th century four-story structure. The locals call this building the "House of the Jew." A plaque on the wall of the building reads, "SAL/OMON/HEBR." This was the house of Salomone di Gaglio, who built this house in 1410. His house was used as a bank and Jewish community center. The surname "Olivetti," according to some scholars, is derived from "di Oliveto," coming from Oliveto.

Great Synagogue of Modena.

PARMA

SYNAGOGUE Vicolo Cervi #4 Tel. (0521) 774 823

The Jews of Parma were expelled in 1555. They returned two centuries later. The synagogue was built in 1866 and follows the Italian ritual. The Ark was removed from the 18th century synagogue in Colorno. The building was recently restored. It is used only on major Jewish holidays. In 1881, there were 510 Jews living in Parma. Today, there are about 30.

JEWISH CEMETERY Viale della Villetta

There are two tombstones of Jewish soldiers; one Italian, the other Austrian. They were enemies during World War I, but have been placed next to each other in death.

PALATINA LIBRARY Piazza della Pace

This library contains a collection of ancient Hebrew manuscripts and Bibles.

REGGIO EMILIA

GHETTO SITE

The ghetto was instituted in 1671. It was located along four parallel streets: Via Monzermone, Via Aquila, Via della Volta, and Via Cagiati, and was intersected by Via Emilia and Via Roco. There was a large yeshiva in the city, which was headed by Rabbis Beniamino Vitale and Isaia Bassano. Rabbi Jacob Israel Carni was an active participant in Napoleon's "Sanhedrin" in 1806.

ANCIENT SYNAGOGUE Via dell 'Aquila #4

This Italian ritual congregation conducted its last services in 1858. The Ark was shipped to the Kiryat Shmuel Synagogue in Haifa, in the 1950s.

JEWISH CEMETERY Via della Canalina

1756 marble Ark from Reggio Emilia is now housed in the Central Synagogue of Kiryat Shmuel in Haifa, Israel.

SCANDIANO

GHETTO SITE Via Frumentaria

For information about visiting the cemeteries in this area, contact the Community Center in Modena at (059) 223978.

SORAGNA

A small group of Jews settled in Soragna toward the beginning of the 16th century. They enjoyed many liberties. They were permitted to purchase land and homes. They were the only Jews in the Parmese area who did not have to live in a ghetto. There were, however, several anti-Jewish events. In 1791, Lazzaro Fano covered an image of the Madonna, which was on the façade of his house. He was driven out of town. In 1815, a satirical comedy about the customs of the Jews was written by Giuseppe Motta and performed with marionettes in the Theater of Soragna. The Jews protested and, by order of the Magistrate of Soragna, Pietro Tommasini publicly denounced the program.

Jews were required to pay 40 pieces of gold and two jugs of wine to the gatekeeper, as funerals passed from the synagogue, through the city gate, and then to the cemetery.

SYNAGOGUE and MUSEUM Via Cavour #43 Tel. (0524) 69104

The 16th century synagogue was rebuilt in 1855. It followed the Italian ritual. The building was used as headquarters for the Fascist regime in Soragna during the Second World War. It was restored in 1982 and now contains a synagogue, which is used only for special occasions, and a Jewish Museum. The museum is divided into five sections. There are historical documents which refer to the Jewish communities in the Province of Parma from 1555 to 1803.

The original 16th century Ark was removed and sent to Israel in 1966. It is located in the synagogue of the Knesset, the Israeli Parliament, in Jerusalem. In 1972, Israel issued a series of four anniversary stamps with images of the furnishings of Italian synagogues, including those of Ancona, Padua, Reggio Emilia, and Soragna.

JEWISH CEMETERY Via degli Israeliti

The original cemetery was located in the "Bresciana" estate, which is today located behind the Locanda del Lupo (Wolf's Inn). The newest cemetery is located on the road leading to Fidenza, in Villa Argine, about 3 km outside of town.

17th century Ark from Soragna, presently in the synagogue of the Knesset in Jerusalem.

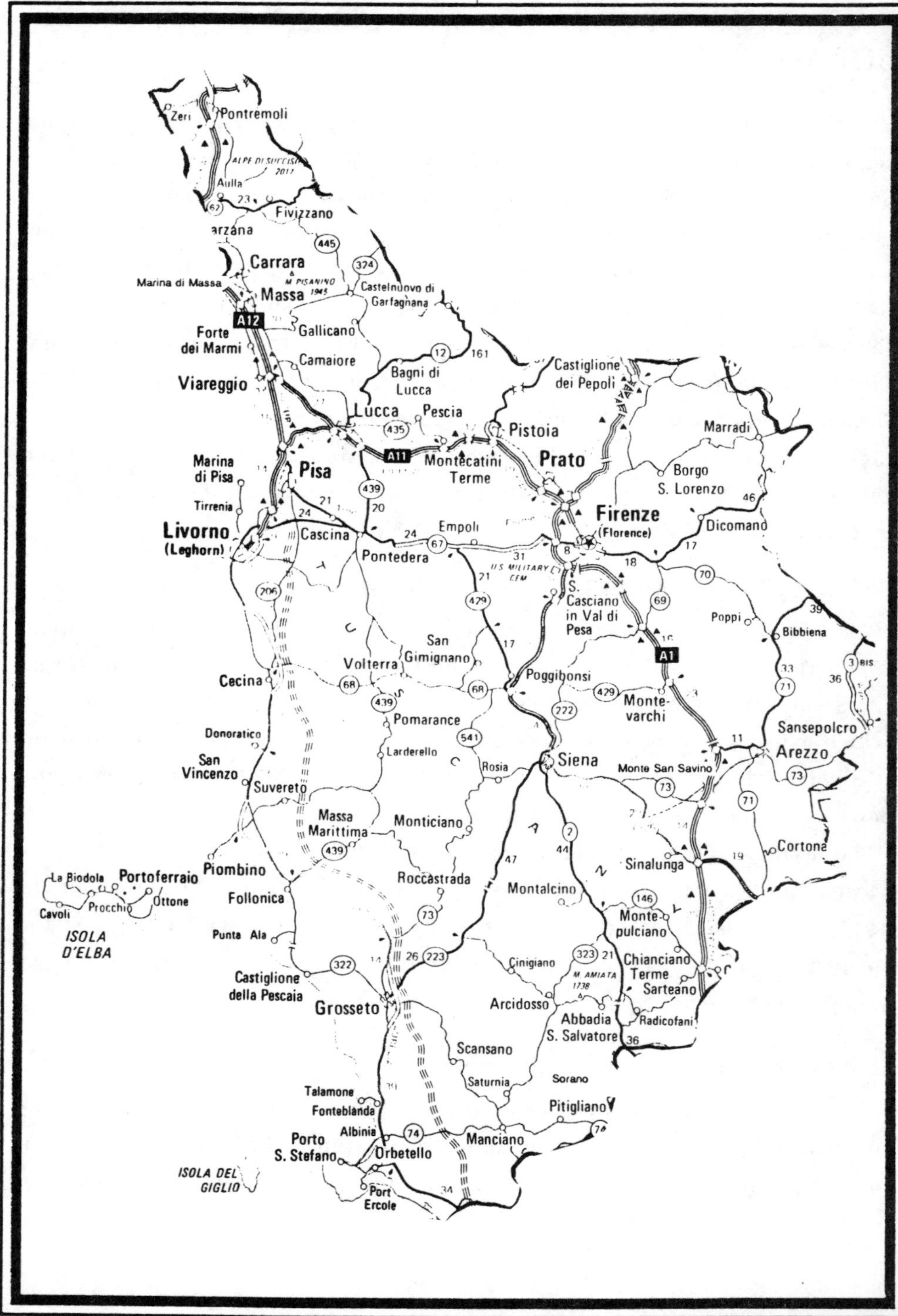

Zeri
Pontremoli
Aulla
Fivizzano
Carrara
Marina di Massa
Massa
Castelnuovo di Garfagnana
A12
Gallicano
Forte dei Marmi
Camaiore
Viareggio
Bagni di Lucca
Castiglione dei Pepoli
Lucca
Pescia
Pistoia
Marradi
A11
Montecatini Terme
Prato
Marina di Pisa
Pisa
Borgo S. Lorenzo
Tirrenia
Firenze
(Florence)
Dicomano
Livorno
(Leghorn)
Cascina
Empoli
Pontedera
S. Casciano in Val di Pesa
Poppi
Bibbiena
San Gimignano
A1
Volterra
Poggibonsi
Cecina
Montevarchi
Pomarance
Sansepolcro
Donoratico
Larderello
Arezzo
San Vincenzo
Rosia
Siena
Monte San Savino
Suvereto
Massa Marittima
Monticiano
Cortona
Piombino
Sinalunga
La Biodola
Portoferraio
Roccastrada
Montalcino
Cavoli
Procchio
Ottone
Follonica
Montepulciano
ISOLA D'ELBA
Punta Ala
Cinigiano
Chianciano Terme
Castiglione della Pescaia
Sarteano
Grosseto
Arcidosso
Abbadia S. Salvatore
Radicofani
Scansano
Saturnia
Sorano
Talamone
Fonteblanda
Pitigliano
Albinia
Porto S. Stefano
Manciano
Orbetello
ISOLA DEL GIGLIO
Port Ercole

Tuscany Region

Benjamin of Tudela encountered the Jewish communities of Florence, Pisa, Lucca, and Siena during his travels through Italy in 1159. At the beginning of the 15th century, there were small Jewish centers in Pescia, Prato, Colle Val d'Elsa, Arezzo, Montepulciano, Castiglione Fiorentino, Volterra, Castrocaro, and Empoli.

The Jews continued to enjoy the protection of the Medici family in 1555, except in Lucca, Massa Carrara, and the Presidi state. In 1570, Duke Cosimo I imposed a law confining the Jews of Florence and Siena in ghettos. Many Jews left the region at this time and the small communities vanished.

In 1593, Grand Duke Ferdinand I invited the *marranos* from Portugal. They established communities in Livorno and Pisa. This "Livornina" did not require the Jews to live in a ghetto. Thousands of Jews from nearby provinces, therefore, settled and lived freely in Livorno and Pisa.

A different situation occurred with the Jewish community of Pitigliano. The Jews who were fleeing from the Papal State arrived in this city in the 16th century. They settled in this city, which is situated on the border of the Lazio and Tuscany regions. They lived an isolated life, segregated from the other communities and were always hoping to return to their places of origin.

In the 17th century, some Jews returned to Arezzo. Others went to Monte San Savino and Borgo San Sepolcro. These small Jewish settlements survived for another century. In 1799, some communities were totally wiped out by the troops of the *Viva Maria.* The number of Jews living in the Tuscany region diminished steadily after the creation of the Kingdom of Italy in 1861. Today, there are organized Jewish communities in Florence, Pisa, Livorno, and Siena.

FLORENCE (Firenze)

In 1430, the Medici family invited four Jewish families (the Pisas, Tivolis, Rietis, and the Fanos) to settle in the city and practice moneylending. The Jews had to submit to precise specifications and work with fixed taxes, which were set by the rulers. These taxes were lower than what the Florentine bankers had been charging.

Lorenzo Medici (1449-1492) invited several Jewish humanists to his Court, such as Jochanan Alemanno, Abraham Farissol, and Elia Delmedigo. Delmedigo was a disciple of Pico della Mirandola. His prestige is shown by his accompanying of the Medici family in the famous fresco of the Palazzo Medici Riccardo (Via Cavour #1). The fresco, painted by Benozzo Gozzoli, represents the "Adoration of the Magi," but in reality, depicts and exalts the Medici Court, in all its pomp and splendor. Delmedigo is among the group of wise men.

The Florentine Jews experienced their first persecutions when Girolamo Savonarola began to preach against them in the city. There were partial expulsions in 1477 and in 1491. A general expulsion in 1495 was averted thanks to the enormous loan that the Jews made to the Republic. The threat, however, was repeated in 1527. The unification of the Duchy created a civil and peaceful life for the Jews.

In 1551, the Medicis invited a large group of Jews from Spain and Portugal. This invitation was primarily due to the advice given by Jacob Abrabanel. They were capable businessmen and would develop trade with Middle East countries. They were also familiar with the nuances, customs, and languages of the many Jewish contacts in other countries.

The same Cosimo wished to obtain the crown of Grand Duke from Pope Pius V. He therefore, did not hesitate to sacrifice the liberties of the Jews, who until then, had always been defended by his family. In 1567, he forced the Jews to wear the identification mark. In 1571, the Jews were forced into the ghetto.

All of the Jews in the surrounding towns of San Miniato, San Giminiano, Volterra, and Monte San Savino, had to move into the ghetto of Florence. Only some wealthy families managed to remain outside of the ghetto. They continued to live near the Palazzo Pitti, on Via dei Giudei (now Via dei Ramaglianti), where the Medicis could easily go to get loans. This was the first street in Florence to be inhabited by Jews. It once had a synagogue.

In 1738, the City of Florence (as well as the entire Region of Tuscany) was passed over to the Lorena family. Grand Duke Leopold I (1765-90) granted the Jews their first civil rights. The Jews were therefore indifferent to the arrival of Napoleon. They did not suffer during the Restoration because the Lorenas, who returned to power, did not change their benevolent attitude toward the Jews.

The golden period for Florentine Jews was between the end of the 19th and early 20th centuries. In 1882, the Great Synagogue was built and the old ghetto was razed to the ground. In 1889, the Rabbinical College was inaugurated. It was headed by Rabbi Samuel Hirsch Marguleis. He was the religious leader of the community for 32 years (1890-1922).

Many Jewish magazines and newspapers were published during this period, including the"Jewish Magazine," "Jewish Weekly," and the"Jewish Monthly Review."

In 1931, there were 2,700 Jews in Florence. During the Nazi period, 248 Jews were deported. Rabbi Nathan Cassuto, the leader of the Jewish community, was among the deportees. The Hebrew school and a street have been named in his memory. There were 1,600 Jews in Florence following the war. Today, there are about 1,200 Jews in the city.

GHETTO SITE Piazza della Repubblica

The ghetto was created in 1571. It extended from the present Piazza della Repubblica to the Piazza dell 'Olio, between Via Roma and Via Brunelleschi. It was located in the run-down market area, known as the "Frascato." The ghetto buildings were redesigned by architect Bernardo Buontalenti. He linked all of the old buildings in the area into one single structure. There were three portals which were equipped with gates.

There were several small palazzi (villas), which had belonged to patrician families such as the Pecoraris, Tosinghis, della Tosas, Medicis, and the Brunelleschis, The wealthier Jewish families settled in these mansions, while the poorer Jewish families inhabited the decaying and unsanitary older buildings.

The interior of this incredible block of buildings consisted of a tightly woven network of small roads, courtyards, arcades, etc., which created a labyrinth. The center of this maze was called the Piazza of the Ghetto.

They were not permitted to work with wool or silk, nor were they permitted to deal with jewels or valuables. Only some of the more privileged Jews were given concessions for non-essential goods, such as brandy and tobacco.

There were two synagogues in the ghetto. One followed the Italian ritual while the other followed the Spanish ritual. The two congregations were moved to Via della Oche #5 in 1884, after the Great Synagogue was inaugurated. They were subsequently shipped to Israel in the 1960s. The furnishings of the Italian Synagogue were sent to the Yad Hagiborim Synagogue, in Ramat Gan. The furnishings of the Spanish Synagogue were sent to the Yeshiva Kerem be-Yavneh.

The ghetto was dismantled in 1848, 278 years after it was instituted. It was razed to the ground between 1881 and 1898, as part of an urban renewal project for the center of the city. There is a plaque in the Piazza della Repubblica which records this event.

BASILICA of SAN CROCE Piazza San Croce

In 1860, it was decided to enrich the façade of the Basilica with marble bandings. The commission was given to architect Nicolo Matas. His contract stipulated that no work was to be performed on Saturdays. The priests were never aware that he was a Jew, of Anconan origin. Nicolo Matas placed a large Star of David on the façade of the Basilica, as a decorative motif.

When Matas died, he embarrassed both the Jewish community and the Franciscan Order. His contract with the Basilica stipulated that he would be buried within the Basilica. A compromise was reached. Matas is now entombed in a marble sarcophagus outside of the Basilica, under a set of stairs, leading into the main entrance.

GREAT SYNAGOGUE Via L.C. Farini #4 Tel. (055) 245 252

The first stone was laid in 1874. It came from Jerusalem. Eight years later, the magnificent Moorish-style synagogue was inaugurated. It was designed by architects Marco Treves, Mariano Falcini, and Vincenzo Micheli, at a cost of approximately one million Lire. The building is designed with alternating bands of white and pink stone, coming from the region of Colle val d'Elsa and Assisi. Its main exterior feature is its magnificent copper dome.

There is a beautiful English garden in the courtyard which surrounds the synagogue. The entire interior of the synagogue is decorated with mosaics and frescos. The color scheme is gold, on blue background. It was designed by artist Giovanni Panti. The main hall opens up under a magnificent cupola. The

19th century Ark of the Tempio Italiano of Florence, now in the Yad Giborim Synagogue in Ramat Gan, Israel.

women's balcony is supported by lavish Moorish arches and marble columns. The congregation follows the Spanish ritual.

The Ark is recessed in an apse and is designed with gold mosaics. It is supported by four black marble columns. There are several ax marks on the doors of the Ark. This was done during the Second World War, by the Nazis. The Tevah is located in the front section of the synagogue. The rabbi's pulpit is situated on a raised platform and is reached by a winding staircase.

The synagogue was restored several times during its history. Two years following its inauguration, it was repaired for major structural problems. The building was settling too rapidly. During World War II, the Nazis set up mines throughout the building, which damaged its stability. In 1966, the waters of the Arno River overflowed. On November 4 of that year, the water level reached 3 meters on the outside of the synagogue and flooded the interior with 2 meters of

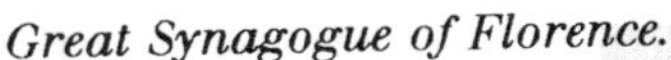

Great Synagogue of Florence.

water. Ninety of the 120 Torahs were seriously damaged. The library, which contained 15,000 volumes, was also damaged. There are several historic plaques located in the vestibule which record the visits by King Victor Emanuel III, King Umberto and Queen Margherita.

The Jewish Museum is located on the third floor of the building. It contains ancient ritual objects, precious brocaded vestments, and photographs of the former synagogues in Florence. The museum is open from October 1 through April 30 on Sundays, Mondays, and Wednesdays, from 10 a.m. to 1 p.m. From May 1 through September 30, the museum is open on Sundays and Thursdays, from 9 a.m. to 1 p.m. and on Mondays and Wednesdays, from 9 a.m. to 1 p.m. and from 2 to 5 p.m.

The Hebrew school and Jewish Rest Home are located within the synagogue courtyard. There is a small daily chapel, which follows the Ashkenazic ritual, located in the Hebrew school. There is also a mikveh in this complex.

JEWISH CEMETERY Via Ariosto #14

The modern Jewish cemetery is located on Via Caciolle #13. The original cemetery, dating from the 18th century, is located on Via Ariosto #14. For further information, call 416 723.

KOSHER RESTAURANT

IL CUSCUSSU Via L.C. Farini 2/A Tel. 241890

KOSHER BUTCHERS

BIGAZZI di PIETRO FALSETTINI Tel. 666 549

A.CAPELLI Via dei Macci #106 Tel. 666 534

LIVORNO

On June 10, 1593, Grand Duke Ferdinand I de 'Medici invited "all merchants of any nation" to settle in Livorno and Pisa. This invitation was known as the "Livornina," and was directed toward the *marranos* in Portugal. They were expelled from Spain in 1492 and moved to nearby Portugal. Portugal, in turn, expelled these Jews. Some of them converted to Christianity in public, but retained their Jewish identities in private. These were the *marranos,* or secret Jews.

In 1548, Cosimo I had invited the *marranos*, but had little success. In 1593, they did accept the invitation issued by Ferdinand I. He offered them freedom of trade and religion and protection from the Inquisition. The Medici's motives were purely economic. They wanted to develop Livorno, which, until then, was a small town of only 1,500 residents. It concentrated largely on the spice trade. It received spices from the East and redistributed them throughout Europe. The new port was to serve as an outlet for the Tuscan textile industry which was just developing.

In 1601, 114 Portuguese Jews arrived in Livorno. It increased to 711 in 1622, to 3,000 in 1689, to 4,300 in 1784, and to 5,000 in 1800. Jews also arrived from central Italy, fleeing from the Papal State.

Spanish became the official language of the community. It was also the dominant ritual in the synagogue. The "bagito" dialect, a mixture of Spanish, Italian, and Hebrew, was born. It was used in poetic compositions and is still spoken by a few elderly members of the community.

The new arrivals did not automatically become Tuscan subjects because of the "Livornina." They had to be "voted upon" by the elders of the community. They would either accept them or not and would send them to either Livorno or Pisa.

Livorno was a cosmopolitan community, where the Middle Easterners, Turks, and Africans lived in a climate of extreme tolerance. In 1614, Livorno broke away from the mother-community of Pisa. It became an autonomous city.

The Jews were concentrated in the area around the castle, where no Christians lived. Despite this voluntary separation, there was never a ghetto in the city. The principal road in the Jewish quarter was Via Grande. The Jewish soap factory was on Via Saponiera. The wealthier Jews lived on Via Reale. The entire area was rebuilt in 1908. Many of the buildings, including the first synagogue, were demolished, as part of an urban improvement project.

The Livornese Jews were mostly businessmen. They owned one third of the stores in the city in 1765. They later built small factories for the production of soap, paper, and coral designs. Some families branched out to Tripoli, Egypt, and Tunisia in order to facilitate their own commercial houses.

There were six Hebrew Academies (yeshivot) in Livorno between the 16th and 18th centuries. Joseph Ergas, Malachi ben Jacob ha-Kohen, Hezekiah de Silva, and Emanuel Hay Ricchi were among the most notable scholars in Livorno. The noted Cabbalist, Elia Benamozegh (1823-1900), studied in Livorno. The street in front of the synagogue has been named in his honor.

Former Great Synagogue at Livorno.

16th century Ark from Livorno now located near the Yochanan ben Zakai synagogue complex in Jerusalem.

Livorno was severely damaged by the arrival of Napoleon. He blocked the port. Livorno was no longer a "Free Port." This destroyed the economy of the city. Many Jews left. The Jewish population dropped from 4,500 in 1852 to 2,500 in 1900. During the war, 90 Jews were deported by the Nazis. In 1965, the Jewish population was 650. After the Six Day War, 150 Libyan Jews were forced to leave their homeland. They settled in Livorno. Today, there are approximately 750 Jews in the city.

SYNAGOGUE Piazza Benamozegh #1 Tel. (0586) 24290

The most beautiful synagogue in Italy was built on this site in 1591. It was enlarged and embellished over the next three hundred years. It was totally destroyed during an aerial bombing attack on the city during World War II. The present synagogue was built on the same site in 1962. It was designed by architect Angelo Di Castro.

The modern structure is made of precast concrete and resembles the *succah* of ancient times. The main sanctuary is designed as an amphitheater and is elliptical in shape. The Ark is located in the back-center of the hall. It was removed from the former Spanish Synagogue in Pesaro, in 1970. The 18th century gilded Ark is designed in the Baroque style. Two columns flank the doors of the Ark. There is a large corona, composed of gilded wooden garlands on the upper portion of the Ark.

The main sanctuary, which follows the Spanish ritual, is used only on major Jewish holidays. The Lampront Chapel, housed in the basement of the synagogue, is used for daily services. The furnishings of this Spanish-ritual chapel, have been removed from the former Spanish Synagogue in Ferrara. There is a memorial plaque dedicated to the noted philanthropist, Sir Moses Montefiore, who was born in Livorno in 1785.

The Community Center, Hebrew school, and mikveh are housed in the adjoining building. The entrance is located at Corso Mazzini #3.

MARINI YESHIVA Via Micali

The Ark was brought to Livorno by Portuguese immigrants in the 15th century. It is made from gilded wood and is carved with floral designs. It is capped with three pinnacled cupolas.

JEWISH CEMETERY Via Fabio Filzi

The oldest Jewish cemetery in Livorno was located on the Lungomare, near the Mulinacci beach. It was moved to Via Pompilia, in front of the Fortress, in 1648. It remained there until 1734. Another cemetery was in use from 1694, and was located on Via Corallo. It was closed in 1941. The present Lupi Cemetery is located on Via Fabio Filzi.

MARINA di MASSA

There is a parish church which is dedicated to San Dominichino, the child from Zaragoza, whose death was attributed to Jewish ritual murder, in 1240. The martyrdom is solemnly remembered in August. The cult was introduced to this city in 1957, when the remains of the child were brought from Spain. The church is located on the Contrada Ronchi. There is a fresco which recalls the episode.

MONTE SAN SAVINO

GHETTO SITE Via del Ghetto

HOUSE of the RABBI (Casa del Rabbino) Via del Ghetto #11

The Jews in this city were massacred by the *Viva Maria* troops in 1799, in the Piazza Jalta.

PISA

When Benjamin of Tudela visited Pisa in 1165, he found twenty Jews in the city. In the beginning of the 1300s, the Jews were required to live in a separate section of town and had to wear the special identification mark. These restrictions, however, did not last very long. In the mid 1300s, the City of Pisa invited Jews to settle in their city. The invitation was extended to a Roman group, which included the family of Vitale de Matassia da Roma. He became the most important Jewish banker during the Renaissance. He was protected by the Medici family. Vitale soon took the surname of Da Pisa.

The Da Pisa family maintained their connections with other Jewish communities scattered throughout Tuscany, the rest of Italy, and the entire

Leaning Tower of Pisa.

Mediterranean. These connections were familial, religious, cultural, and financial. They hosted relatives, friends, and scholars from throughout the Mediterranean. These men studied Talmudic and Cabbalistic tractates. The pseudo-Messiah, David ha-Reuveni (died ca. 1538), visited the Da Pisas.

In 1492, many Jews arrived from Spain. They became door-to-door clothes salesmen. They carried their wares in bundles on their backs or in hand-pulled carts. The Da Pisa family helped and protected these peddlers.

The Medicis wanted Pisa to become a commercial emporium, with Livorno as its seaport. They invited the *marranos* from Portugal to help develop this plan. More than 500 Jews arrived from Portugal. The small existing Jewish community was absorbed by the new arrivals. The Portuguese Jews imposed their traditions, rituals, language (a mix of Spanish, Hebrew and Portuguese), and even their style of dress. Many, in fact, retained their turbans.

The San Andrea area became the Jewish quarter of the city. There was never a ghetto in Pisa. In 1600, there were 600 Jews living in Pisa. By 1881, the population reached its peak, with 700 Jews. They were involved in the textile (cotton) industries. During the Second World War, a dozen Jews were deported, including the leader of the Jewish community for thirty-two years, Rabbi Augusto Hasda. Today, there are about 185 Jews living in Pisa.

19th century Ark from Pisa, now housed in the synagogue of Machon Gold, Jerusalem.

SYNAGOGUE Via Palestro #24 Tel. (050) 27269

The synagogue structure was built in 1595. It was remodeled in 1785, 1865, and in the early 1900s. The interior contains the community offices, a former Hebrew school, mikveh, and matzoh factory. The main sanctuary is designed in the Classical style. The Tevah is designed in walnut and is circular in shape.

HOUSE of the JEWS (Casa degli ebrei) Via Domenico Cavalca #36

This large mansion, located in the center of the city, was the home of Vitale de Matassia Da Pisa. It also served as his bank and synagogue. He had another mansion in Asciano,which could be reached by waterway.

HOME of GIUSEPPE PARDO ROQUES Via San Andrea

Giuseppe Pardo Roques was a noted member and president of the Jewish community. On August 1, 1944, the Nazis stormed into his house and killed Roques and six other Jews who were hidden in his house. There is a memorial plaque on the façade of the house. A street was named in his honor. A painting by Bertolini was commissioned in memory of this massacre. It is hanging in the lobby of the synagogue.

JEWISH CEMETERY Piazza del Duomo

The first Jewish cemetery (1163-1330) is located just outside of the medieval wall, near the Piazza del Duomo - near the Leaning Tower of Pisa. There was a second cemetery created in 1603. It was removed in 1674 and replaced with the cemetery to the right of the Porta Nuovo.

PITIGLIANO

Pitigliano became the first refuge for Jews fleeing from the Papal State, in 1569 and again in 1593. Many Jews stopped here, thinking of returning as soon as the opportunity arose. This opportunity did not come for a long time. Pitigliano was a small oasis of tranquility. It was protected by the Medicis and the Lorenas. The Jews were involved in trade and agriculture. There was a large matzoh factory. All of the women in the Jewish community worked in this factory. There was a kosher butcher who furnished meat to many non-Jews. They believed that since the meat was kosher, it must have come from healthy animals. The non-Jewish farmers and the Jews worked side by side in the fields. The farmers went to the

The synagogue of Carmiel (Israel) houses the 18th century Ark from Pitigliano.

Jewish elders of the community when they needed technical or legal advice.

Pitigliano was the birthplace of many distinguished sages and scholars, including Dante Lattes, Samuel Colombo (who was the rabbi of Livorno), the biologist, Mazzini Pergola, and Ugo Sorani, the vice president of the House of Deputies and the Undersecretary of the Ministry of Justice. The community disintegrated in 1799, with the invasion of Napoleon and the subsequent attacks by the *Viva Maria* troops.

GHETTO SITE Piazza Petrucciolo

ANCIENT SYNAGOGUE Via Zuccarelli

JEWISH CEMETERY

Contact the Community Center in Livorno at (0586) 28722.

Note: An excellent kosher wine is now produced in Pitigliano.

SIENA

GHETTO SITE Piazza del Campo

The first Jews arrived in Siena during the 13th century. In 1493, the Jews were required to wear the identification mark, which consisted of a yellow cord made into a circular shape, and sewn onto the overcoat. The ghetto was created in 1571.

Siena was known as the "Little Jerusalem." There were five great Hebrew academies in the end of the 19th century. The French occupied the city in 1796 and burned the doors of the ghetto. In 1799, when Napoleon was in Egypt, the supporters of the Lorena family initiated revolts against the French. The revolts were led by Giuseppe Romanelli di Quaranta and were aided by the Austro-Russian armies. These revolutionaries were called *Viva Marias.*

The *Viva Marias* departed from Arezzo and sacked the entire countryside. On June 28, 1799, they devastated the ghetto and pillaged the shops. The synagogue was attacked. The doors of the Ark still bear the scars of this event. In 1935, many of the old buildings in the ghetto area were demolished as part of the urban renewal plan of Siena.

Synagogue of Siena was built in 1756.

ובהיכלו כלו אמר
כבוד

SYNAGOGUE Via delle Scotte #14 Tel. (0577) 284 647

The synagogue, built in 1756, was designed in the Neo-Classical style by architect Giuseppe del Rosso. Its design was influenced by Vanvitelli, who also worked in Siena. The plaque in the vestibule records the visit by the Grand Duke of Tuscany, Leopold II, and Maria Antonio of Naples in 1823. The elaborate wooden decorations in the synagogue were designed by Nicolo Iande and Pietro Rossi. The Corinthian marble columns flanking the Ark are said to have come from Jerusalem.

The synagogue, which follows the Italian ritual, conducts services only on the Sabbath and on major Jewish holidays. The "Fountain of the Ghetto," is located opposite the synagogue. In the 16th century, the fountain was adorned with a statue of Moses pointing down to the water. It was said to have been designed by Jacopo della Quercia. It was removed in 1875, when several Orthodox Jews from Poland claimed that the statue represented a "graven image" which was a blatant violation of the Torah. The statue is presently on display in the Community Museum.

JEWISH CEMETERY Via Certosa

STATE ARCHIVES Via Banchi di Sotto #10

There are many documents and manuscripts which deal with the Jewish history of Siena in the State Archives.

SORANO

GHETTO SITE Via del Ghetto

ANCIENT SYNAGOGUE

The ancient synagogue is located within the old ghetto site and is presently a ceramics shop.

VIAREGGIO

This is a summer resort community. There is a small synagogue and a kosher restaurant. The synagogue is located at Via degli Oleandri #30. The kosher restaurant is located in the Grand Hotel Principe di Piedmont. Inquire at Via Bertini (Giulio Arieti) Tel. 51327.

Medieval Jews of Italy.

San Marino
Pennabilli
Pesaro
A14
Fano
16
423
Urbino
BIS.
73
Urbania
Fossombrone
73
Marotta
Senigallia
Marzocca
Cagli
424
M. CATRIA
1704
Pergola
360
Arcevia
Iesi
Ancona
Porto Novo
Sassoferrato
76
362
Osimo
Numana
Fabriano
Cingoli
Loreto
Recanati
Porto Recanati
Galdo Tadino
502
77
Matelica
Macerata
Civitanova Marche
256
Camerino
Tolentino
Muccia
77
Corridonia
A14
Porto S. Giorgio
S. Ginesio
Montegiorgio
Fermo
Sarnano
210
Visso
Pedaso
Amandola
78
Grottammare
M. VETTORE
2476
Ascoli Piceno
S. Benedetto del Tronto

Marche Region

There were Jews living in this region as early as the 3rd century. They were involved in moneylending and settled in cities which were important centers of commerce with the Middle East. This region was under the rule of the Papal State. During the 15th and 16th centuries, the number of banks increased. There were Jewish-run banks in Fano, Pesaro, Fossombrone, Cagli, Civitanova, Roccacontrada, Montebodio, Osimo, Fabriano, Montesecco, Castelfidardo, Mondavico, Cingoli, Montelupone, Iesi, Casteldurante, Macerata, Camerino, San Angelo in Vado, and Senigallia. This is only a partial list.

The papal bulls of 1555 and 1569, forced the Jews to live in a ghetto. Over fifty small Jewish communities vanished as a direct result of these edicts. The only ghetto in the entire region was located in Ancona. Several thousand Jews moved into this ghetto. Some Jews moved out of the region and settled in northern Italy, Istanbul, Smirne, Salonika, and Jerusalem. All that remains of the former Jewish communities are street names such as *Via degli ebrei*. Some Jews used the name of their town as their surname. From the mid-1500s, the Jews in the Marche region lived only in Ancona, Urbino, Pesaro, and Senigallia.

ANCONA

Jews arrived in Ancona around the year 1000. The community grew rapidly. In 1300, Ancona was second only to Rome in Jewish population. It was one of the principal Rabbinical seats in central Italy. Many merchants were attracted to Ancona's important port. It had strong commercial ties with the Levant (Middle East).

GHETTO SITE Via Astagno

Ancona was a subject of the Papal State since 1532. In 1555, the ghetto was instituted. It was the only ghetto in the entire Marche region. All of the Jews from the small towns in the countryside were expelled at this time. They were all forced to move into this one ghetto.

The Popes were in control of the lives of the Jews. Pope Paul III protected the Jews and encouraged their settlement. Pope Paul IV forced them to live in the ghetto and required the Jews to wear the identification mark (a hoop in the ear for women, a yellow circle on the coats, for the men). In 1556, twenty five *marranos* refused to renounce their faith. Pope Paul IV brought them to the Piazza Enrico Malatesta and had them burned to death.

Italian Synagogue of Ancona.

17th century Ark from Ancona, presently located in the Tel Aviv University Synagogue.

This tragic episode shook the Jewish communities throughout the Mediterranean basin and mobilized them in defense of their persecuted co-religionists. A commercial boycott was decreed against the Port of Ancona. Even Suleiman the Magnificent joined this boycott. All of the trade controlled by the Jews was moved to the nearby Port of Pesaro. This protest lasted two years and was the first gesture of organized defense for the Jews against excessive powers of the papacy.

The Jews of Ancona asked for the boycott to be terminated. They were afraid of Papal reprisals. This tragic episode was remembered (until recently) with a special prayer of atonement which was recited on *Tish'a Ba'Av* (the ninth day of the Hebrew month of Av, which commemorates the destruction of the Holy Temples in Jerusalem).

The ghetto was dismantled in 1796. Three Jews, Sanson Constantini, David and Ezechial Morpurgo, were elected to the new community council. A year later, however, the ghetto was reinstated. Thirty years passed until the ghetto was again dismantled. This time it was permanent.

At the beginning of the 20th century, there were 1,800 Jews living in Ancona. Today, there are only about 200.

SYNAGOGUE Via Astagno #12 Tel. (071) 202 638

This building was designed for the Levantine Synagogue. The Italian Synagogue was moved here in 1933. Its former building was demolished. In its place is today's Marchetti Cinema.

The Italian Synagogue is located on the ground floor. It is no longer in use. The Ark is made from gilded wood with etched silver doors. The Levantine Synagogue is located on the first floor of the building. The Tevah was brought from the former synagogue of Pesaro.

JEWISH CEMETERY Monte Cardeto

The old Jewish cemetery has been used since 1428. It is located on top of a mountain, overlooking the sea. The sea has eroded the base of the mountain over the centuries. As a result, many tombstones are sliding toward the sea. The new cemetery is located in Tavernelle.

PESARO

The first records of Jewish settlement date from the year 1200. The community reached its "Golden Age" under the rule of Guidobaldo II della Rovere (1538-74). Gershon Soncino, the noted printer, lived in Pesaro and published the first edition of the *Aruch*, by Nathan ben Yechiel.

Pesaro became the chief port of the region after the embargo was placed on the Port of Ancona, in 1556. After the French armies retreated in 1797, the ghetto and its two synagogues were sacked by the *Viva Maria* troops. From the

The Central Synagogue of Kiryat Zanz houses the 1650 Ark from Pesaro.

beginning of the 19th century, the Jewish population in Pesaro diminished progressively. There were 145 Jews in 1870, 93 in 1901, and today, there is no Jewish community.

GHETTO SITE

The ghetto was located between Via Castelfidardo, Via Sarah Levi Nathan, and Via delle Botteghe.

ANCIENT SYNAGOGUE Via delle Scuole #25

The Italian Synagogue was demolished. The Tevah was sent to Yochanan ben Zakai Synagogue complex in the Old City of Jerusalem. The Spanish Synagogue is presently being restored. The Ark was sent to the synagogue in Livorno. The Tevah was sent to the synagogue in Ancona. The hall is now empty. There were two paintings on the sides of the Tevah, which allegorically represented the old Jerusalem as a female figure immersed in the Marchian countryside.

The ancient Ark from Pesaro (left) has been installed in the modern Great Synagogue of Livorno (above).

JEWISH CEMETERY Via Adriatica

SENIGALLIA

GHETTO SITE Via dei Commercianti

Great markets and fairs were held in this city during the 15th and 16th centuries. The Jews were active as moneylenders. The ghetto was instituted in 1632. The Russian and Turkish troops sacked the ghetto after the Napoleonic rule. In 1833, Sansone Levi was condemned to life imprisonment for subversive activity. The Jewish community virtually ended with the annexation of the Marches by the Kingdom of Italy.

ANCIENT SYNAGOGUE Via dei Commercianti #20

The synagogue is no longer in use. For information, contact the Community Center of Ancona at (071) 202638. The synagogue was built in the 1600s. There was another synagogue on Via Arsilli.

JEWISH CEMETERY Via Grazie #2

The 16th century cemetery was located on Via Capanna. Today, that site is a public garden. The present Jewish cemetery is located on Via Grazie #2, near the Grazie Convent.

URBINO

The first Jews who arrived in Urbino during the 1400s, were of Spanish origin. Frederico da Montefeltro was liberal toward the Jews, and invited them to settle in Urbino and establish businesses. The Jews became so numerous, at one time, that they represented one third of the total population of the city. Jews even sat in the Court of Urbino, acting as advisers to the Duke.

After more than a century of tranquility the situation changed radically. The Duchy was passed to Francesco Maria II della Rovere and became part of the Papal State. The majority of the Jews left when the ghetto was established in 1632, under Pope Urban VIII. The majority of the Jews moved to Pesaro at this time.

The few remaining Jews in Urbino today, depend on Ancona for religious functions and needs.

GHETTO SITE Via Stretta

The ghetto was enclosed with three doors. It extended around Via Stretta, and was closed by Via delle Stallacce on one side, and the medieval wall on the other. The 16th century brick houses are tall and are capped with small turrets.

ANCIENT SYNAGOGUE Via Veterani #12

This former synagogue was located in the upper section of the city. It contained a mikveh and a matzoh factory in the basement. It was closed in 1632, when the Jews were forced to live in the ghetto.

SYNAGOGUE Via Stretta

The synagogue was built in 1633, a year after the ghetto was instituted. The sanctuary is located on the first floor. The hall is rectangular and has a barrel-vaulted ceiling decorated with floral stencils. There are 40 ancient Torahs which are covered with 18th century vestments, in a storage room.

NATIONAL GALLERY of the MARCHES Ducal Palace

The National Gallery contains one of the most significant paintings of the Italian Renaissance, The "Communion of the Apostles." It was painted in 1467 by Paolo Uccello for the Brotherhood of the Corpus Christi. The panels are divided into six scenes: the Sacriligious Transaction; the Desecration of the Host; the Removal of the Miraculous Host; the Pardon of the Lady; the Punishment of the Jew's Family; and the Death of the Christian Woman.

One of these anti-Jewish tales, written before the Black Plague of 1348, tells of a Jew who loaned money to a Christian woman using her clothing as collateral. When she returned to collect her clothing on the day before Easter, the Jew said, "If you bring me the body of your Christ, I will return your clothes to you without charge." The simple woman agreed. After receiving Communion on Easter morning, she returned to the Jew with the Sacrament. The Jew placed the body of Christ in a pot of boiling water. It was not consumed. When several other Christians entered the Jewish pawn shop to borrow money, they saw the desecration of the Host. The Jew was taken away and burned at the stake.

These types of anti-Jewish sermons were preached by the Franciscan priests during this period. In 1468, the Christian-run *Monte di Pieta* were designed to end the Jewish domination of the banks and pawn shops in Urbino.

The synagogue in Urbino was built in 1633.

JEWISH CEMETERY Monte degli ebrei

The Jewish cemetery is located 3 km outside of the city, in the suburb called Gadana. For information about visiting the cemetery and the synagogue, contact the Moscati family at (0722) 4767.

Medieval Italian Jews.

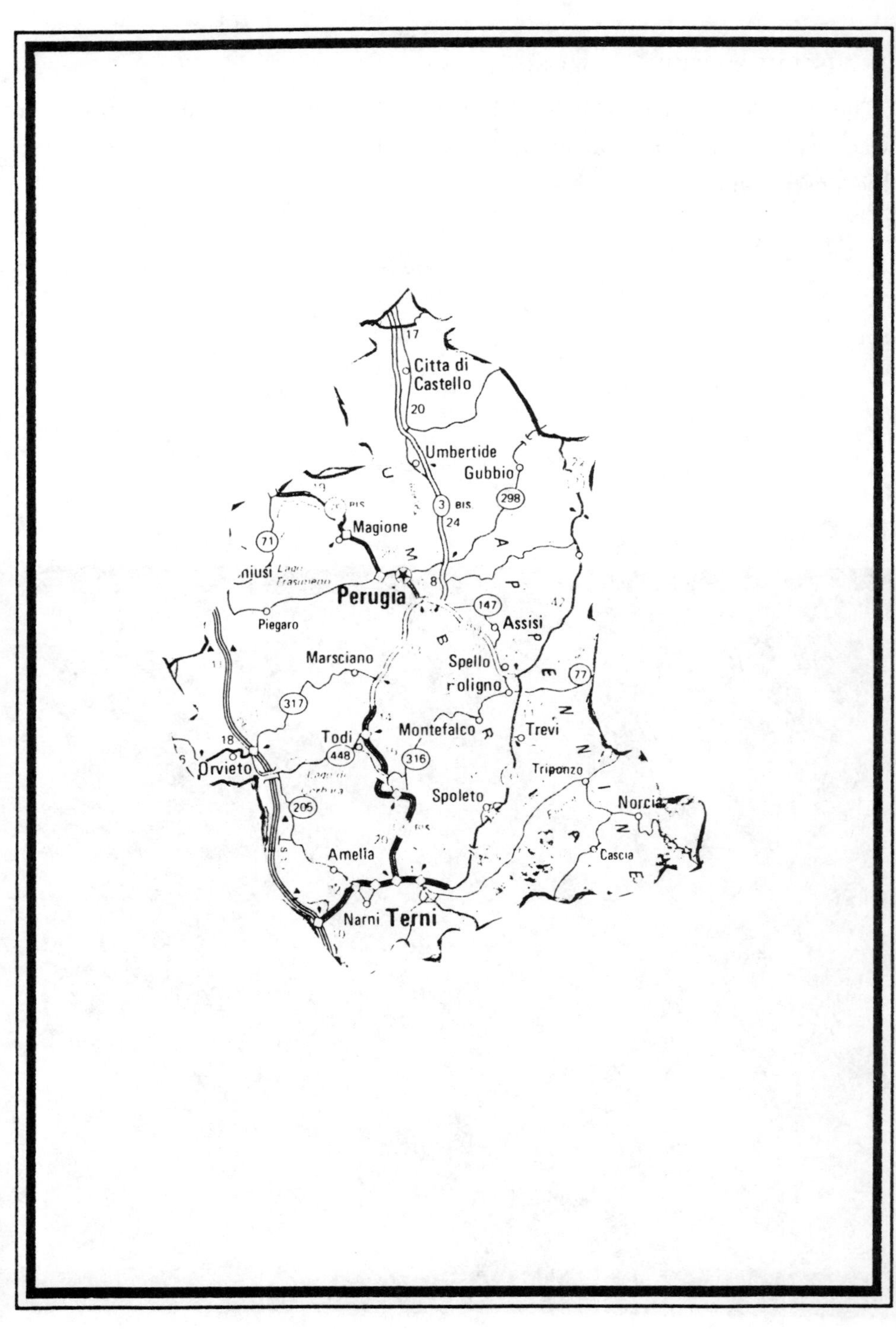

Citta di Castello
Umbertide
Gubbio
Magione
Perugia
Piegaro
Assisi
Marsciano
Spello
Foligno
Montefalco
Trevi
Todi
Orvieto
Triponzo
Spoleto
Norcia
Cascia
Amelia
Narni
Terni

Umbria Region

PERUGIA

In 1367, Guadino di Bonaventura, a Jew, was enrolled in the Medical School. There is nothing left of that early settlement. The present Jewish community depends on the Jewish community of Rome for its religious needs. Religious services are conducted in a private apartment. For information, contact Sergio Pacifici (Via Oberdan #55) at (075) 21250.

SPOLETO

ANCIENT SYNAGOGUE

The ancient synagogue was located on Via San Gregorio della Sinagoga. There are still a few Jews living in this city.

Montalto di Castro
Montefiascone
Civitella d'Agliano
Tuscania
Vitorchiano
Viterbo
Orte
Targuinia
Vetralla
Civita Castellana
Allumiere
Sutri
Tolfa
Bracciano
Sacrofano
A12
A1
Anguillara Sarazia
ROMA (ROME)
Maccarese
Fiumicino
Lido di Ostia
Frascati
Pomezia
Albano Laziale
Tor Vaianica
Aprilia
Anzio
U.S. MILITARY CEM.
Latina
Sabaudia
Circeo Nat'l. Park
M. CIRCEO 541
Terracina
Gaeta
Formia
Minturno
Fondi
Lenola
Fossanova
Priverno
Ceccano
Sezze
Sermoneta
M. SEMPREVISA 1536
Segni
Colleferro
Cori
Velletri
A2
Anagni
Alatri
Frosinone
Fiuggi
Palestrina
Subiaco
A24
Tivoli
Guidonia
Palombara Sabina
Orvinio
Poggio Mirteto
Cottanello
Rieti
Leonessa
Amatrice
Borgorose
Sora
Isola del Liri
Ceprano
Atina
Cassino

Lazio Region

There were Jewish settlements in the following cities before the ghetto in Rome was established in 1555: Acquapendent, Alatri, Anagni, Ariccia, Bagnaia, Castelnuouvo di Porto, Cave, Cori, Frascati, Genazzano, Lanuvio, Marino, Montefiascone, Monte San Giovanni, Nepi, Nettuno, Orte, Palestrina, Priverno, Rieti, Rignano Flaminio, Sezze, Segni, Sernometa, Terracina, Tivoli, Velletri, Veroli, Viterbo, and Vitorchiano. The Jews were expelled from these cities and were forced into the ghettos of Rome and Ancona.

CAMPAGNANO

There was a local legend that told of a treasure which was hidden in the walls of the synagogue. The synagogue was dismantled, stone-by-stone, by the treasure hunters. Alas, no treasure was ever found.

CORI

ANCIENT SYNAGOGUE Piazza Orticara #25

FONDI

The City of Fondi is located along the Appian Way. There was a Jewish settlement in Fondi dating back to the Roman Empire. Fondi was situated along the major trade route from Rome to the Port of Brindisi. There are no further records of Jewish settlement between the 1st and 13th centuries.

Fondi was part of the Kingdom of Naples. The Papal Bulls of expulsion, during the late 16th century, were never carried out in Fondi. The Jewish community, however, did vanish in the middle of the 17th century. The malaria epidemic of 1633 was caused by the use of stagnant waters after a severe drought. The epidemic reduced the general population of Fondi from 10,000 to 332. In a short period of time, the City of Fondi became a deserted moor. This ended the Jewish settlement in Fondi.

ANCIENT JEWISH QUARTER Via dell 'Olmo Perino

The old Jewish quarter was located in the northwest section of the city, in the Portella district, also known as the "Giudea." The Via dell 'Olmo Perino was once called the Via Giudea and was called the Via Ghetto during the Fascist rule. There are no churches in this district. The Jews dealt in textiles and fabric dyeing.

HOUSE of the SPIRITS (Casa degli Spiriti)

This old building, located on the Via dell 'Olmo Perino, is the object of many popular legends. Some say that the house is "possessed" by spirits. It was once part of the Jewish community center and also had a mikveh. It was last used as a house for lepers. It has not been inhabited since the malaria epidemic in 1633.

OSTIA ANTICA

The ancient synagogue was discovered during excavations on the site in 1961. It is the oldest synagogue site in Europe. It is located near the old fluvial embankment. The congregation used the waters of the river for its ritual bath. The complex consisted of a prayer hall, study hall, an oven for baking matzohs, and a hotel.

The 4th century synagogue was built on top of a 1st century synagogue structure. The first building was designed in the *opus vittatum* style, incorporating blocks of volcanic rock (tuff), placed in horizontal rows. The floor of the first level was designed with mosaic tiles, while the floor of the second (4th century) synagogue was designed with marble.

There are three entrances to the synagogue, similar to the ancient synagogues found in the Galilee, in Israel. One door was used as the men's entrance. The second was used by the women, and the third door was the entrance to the mikveh.

Synagogue remains.

The curved back wall of the synagogue was oriented toward the east, in the direction of Jerusalem. The semi-circular niche in the wall housed the Torahs. There are Jewish symbols, such as a Menorah, carved into the architraves.

Note: This archaeological site is closed on Mondays.

PALESTRINA

ANCIENT SYNAGOGUE Contrada Lo Spregato

PRIVERNO

There was a Jewish settlement in this city until the middle of the 19th century.

ROME (Roma)

The Jewish community in Rome is the oldest in the Diaspora. It predates the Holy Roman Empire. The first group of Jews settled in Rome around 139 B.C.E., when Judea, under the rule of Simon Maccabaeus, renewed its pact of allegiance with Rome. The community grew in 61 B.C.E., when Pompeii brought Jewish prisoners from Palestine and sold them as slaves. The number continued to grow with the arrival of itinerant Jewish merchants.

In the year 70, Titus conquered Jerusalem and destroyed the Holy Temple. The Jewish slaves were marched under the Arch of Titus, carrying the spoils of the war, the holy instruments and articles used by the priests in the Holy Temple, including the *Menorah*, *Shulchan,* and trumpets. Many of these Jewish slaves were used in the construction of the Colosseum.

In the first century of the Empire, there were approximately 40,000 to 50,000 Jews in Rome. They lived in the Trastevere section, the Suburra, and in Porta Capena. They organized about thirteen synagogues which were named after their places of origin (Tripoltani, Elea), their neighborhoods (Suburesii, Campesii), or their protectorates (Augustestii, Erodii). Each group had its own internal constitution, autonomy, leaders and teachers, and catacombs and cemeteries.

The oldest synagogue in Europe is found in Ostia Antica. Archaeologists discovered a 4th century synagogue which was built upon an an even earlier

(1st century) structure.

The Jewish religion and the new and evolving Christian religion drew a certain number of converts from the pagan population. The Emperors did not tolerate these actions and condemned the Jews to deportation to Sardinia. When Christianity became the religion of the State in 380, the Jews were persecuted but never completely expelled from Rome. They remained as a testimonial to the ancient roots of the new emerging religion.

The Jewish community was dependent upon the whims of the various popes. Pope Gregory VII confined the Jews in separate quarters in 1215. In 1348, the Jews were accused of spreading the Bubonic Plague by poisoning the wells.

After the Inquisition in Spain, many Jews moved to Rome. Many more came from southern Italy and northern Europe. The existing Jewish community in Rome asked Pope Alexander VI of Borgia not to allow them in the city for they feared that their privileges and conditions might be worsened. They were ready to pay a certain amount of money to the pontiff.

The first half of the 16th century was a period of tolerance. The humanistic Popes included Giulio II della Rovera, Leone X de 'Medici, and Clemente VII de 'Medici. The sermons of the false Messiah, David ha-Reuveni and the *merrano*, Shlomo Molcho, were delivered during the reign of Pope Clemente VII.

On July 14, 1555, Pope Paul IV Carafa issued the Papal Bull,*cum nimis absurdum*. This proclamation instituted the ghetto of Rome. All of the synagogues had to be housed in only one structure. The building, therefore, containing five synagogues was built to facilitate this ruling.

The principle activities in the ghetto were trading used goods and moneylending. There were sixty-four banks in the ghetto. When the *Monte di Pieta* were established in 1692, many of the Jews had to rely on welfare benefits supplied by the Brotherhood of Assistance, which was financed by a few wealthy Jews.

The Jewish community had to pay very high tributes to the Apostolic House and other Christian organizations such as the Catecumens House, which forced Jewish children to convert. At one point, the Jewish community went bankrupt. The Jewish population in 1555 was about 3,000.

There were many public humiliations. The elders of the community had to bring their Torahs to the Arch of Titus and march under it. This Arch was the symbol of Jewish captivity. The crowds would jeer at this processional.

At the end of the 18th century, the French troops, under Napoleon, broke down the ghetto doors. They were put up again, however, after the fall of Napoleon, in 1814. The ghetto was finally dismantled in 1870.

Roman Jews took active roles in national life. In 1871, the House of Deputies had eleven Jewish members, and two Jews were elected as Communal Councilmen. During the First World War, many Jews joined the Italian Army. Jews died on the Italian front, fighting other Jews, on the other side.

During the Nazi occupation of Rome, the Jews returned to a more horrid existence than that experienced in the last years of the ghetto under Pope Pius IX. On October 16, 1943, known as the infamous "Black Saturday," the Nazis rounded up 1,024 Jews. The number reached 2,091 within a week. The elderly, sick, and the children were sent to detention camps. They were then packed into trains and shipped to Dachau, Bergen-Belsen, and Auschwitz. During this period, the Vatican remained silent. From the 2,091 deportees, only 15 returned.

Some young Jews fled to the mountains and joined the partisans. Eugenio and Silvia Elfer were among those Jewish partisans who were captured and killed by the Nazis. The partisans attacked the Nazis on Via Rasella. In retaliation, the Nazis massacred 335 people at the Fosse Ardeatine. There were 73 Jews among the dead.

Leone Ginzburg, the noted scholar of Russian literature, died in prison in 1944. Eugenio Colorni, the philosopher and founder of the European Federalist Movement, was assassinated in Rome in 1944. Enzo Sereni Chajjim, who was the emissary of the Hagganah in Palestine, was captured and killed after being parachuted into northern Italy, while making contact with the Committee for National Liberation.

On June 4, 1944, the Allied troops liberated the City of Rome. Several Jews joined the Allied Forces in pursuit of the retreating Nazis and Fascists. After the war, many Jews emigrated, legally and illegally, to Palestine. There have been isolated incidents of anti-Semitism in Rome such as the tragic attack on the Great Synagogue on Saturday morning, October 9, 1982, in which a small child was killed. The Jewish population of Rome is approximately 15,000.

THE CATACOMBS

The Jews buried their dead during the Common Era, in large underground galleries, similar to the Roman custom. Six Jewish catacombs have been found in Rome. They are located near Gianicolo (Monteverde Catacomb), on the

Appian Way (Catacomb of Vigna Randanini)- near the Basilica of San Sebastiano. This catacomb can be visited. Inquire at the Community Center at (06) 655 051 or 656 4648. There are catacombs on the Via Appia Pignatelli (Vigna Cimarra Catacomb). There are additional catacombs on Via Labicana and on Via Nomentana (Villa Torlonia Catacomb).

ARCH of TITUS

The Arch of Titus is located in the Roman Forum. It depicts, in relief, the Jewish slaves being brought to Rome after the Holy Temple in Jerusalem was destroyed in the year 70. The Jewish slaves are carrying the holy objects which were used by the priests in the Temple, including the *Menorah* and the *Shulchan*.

GHETTO SITE

The ghetto was instituted on July 14, 1555 by Pope Paul IV Carafa. The ghetto was located in the Trastevere section, near the banks of the Tiber River. The ghetto consisted of four buildings which housed an incredible 3,000 people. The boundaries were from the Portico d'Ottavia to the actual banks of the river. When the river flooded, several families were forced to leave their apartments.

The ghetto extended from the Piazza delle Cinque Scuole to the small Church of San Gregorio. The Papal Bull declared that there could only be one synagogue structure in the ghetto. The building of the "Five Synagogues" was therefore created. It housed three Italian ritual congregations (Scola Tempio, Scola Nuova, and Scola Siciliana) and two Spanish ritual congregations (Catalana and Castigliana). The building was almost completely destroyed during a fire in 1893. The surviving furnishings were moved to other synagogues in the city (the Tempio Maggiore, the di Castro Oratory, and the Tempio Spagnolo).

There is an historical plaque on the façade of the Church of San Gregorio. The passage from Isaiah (65:2,3) is inscribed in Latin and Hebrew. It warns the Jews who refuse to convert to Christianity. The Jews were required to attend the sermons in this church. The bridge in front of the church is known as the "Fabricio," or "Bridge of the Four Heads." It was once called the "Jew's Bridge."

GREAT SYNAGOGUE Lungotevere Cenci Tel. 656 4648

The Great Synagogue was inaugurated in 1904. It was designed by architects Costa and Armanni and incorporates Assyrian and Babylonian motifs. There are

Jewish slaves portrayed in the Arch of Titus.

Great Synagogue of Rome.

Ancient ghetto of Rome.

Great Synagogue of Rome.

two small Arks on either side of the central Ark. They are located under the women's galleries and come from the old ghetto. One Ark is from the Scola Siciliana (on the right side). It dates from 1586. The Ark on the left side is a composite of furnishings rebuilt from pieces of various provinces.

On the morning of October 9, 1982, a PLO terrorist drove past the Great Synagogue and fired a machine-gun at the congregation, as it was leaving the Sabbath morning service. A small boy was killed in this attack. Since that attack, the Great Synagogue has been under constant police surveillance.

History was made in this synagogue in 1987, when Pope John Paul II visited. It was the first time in the history of Italian Jewry that a pope visited a Jewish house of worship. The Chief Rabbi of Rome, Dr. E. Toaff, greeted the Pontiff dressed in his white vestments and his tallit.

JEWISH MUSEUM

The Jewish Museum of Rome is located in the building adjoining the Great Synagogue. It contains the permanent collection of the Jewish community. It was inaugurated in 1960. It contains ancient tombstones, religious articles, and manuscripts. The original document declaring the establishment of the ghetto in 1555 is on display. There are rare prayer books, silver objects, Ark curtains, and circumcision chairs.

Note: Be prepared to undergo a thorough security check before entering the Great Synagogue and/or the Jewish Museum of Rome.

JEWISH CEMETERY Verano Cemetery

After the Jews of Rome stopped using catacombs as a burial place, they used a cemetery located near the Porta Portese. During the ghetto period (1555-1870), they used the Aventina Cemetery. The space was very limited, so they superimposed the graves one atop the other, in layers. Mussolini turned this cemetery into the Communal Rosary. A few ancient tombstones are still visible.

The Verano Cemetery is presently used by the Jewish community. It is possible to trace the recent history of Jewish Rome in this cemetery, from the Emancipation, the wars, deportations, peace, various immigrations (of Jews from Tripoli and Russia), and even the painful episode of attacks against the Jews in 1982.

KOSHER PROVISIONS

Da Lisa *Via Joscolo 16 Tel. (6) 704-95-456*
Zi Fenizia *Via Santa Maria del Pianto 64 Tel. 689-6976*
Limentani Settimio Bakery *via Portico d'Ottavio 1*
Pension Carmel *via G. Marneli 11 Tel. 580-9921*

OTHER SYNAGOGUES:

Chabad *Via O. Panciroli 7 Tel. (6) 8632-4176*
Tempio Magiore *Lungotevere Cenci 9 Tel. 684-0061*
Tempio Spagnola *Via Catalana Tel. 656-4648*
Oratorio di Castro *Via Balbo 33 Tel. 475-9881*
Via della Borgata della Magliana Tel. 523-2634
Temple Beth El *Via Padova 92 Tel. 426-160*
Lungotevere Sanzio 12
Via Garefagnana 4 Tel. 424-4521

JEWISH BOOKSTORE

MENORAH Via del Portico d'Ottavia #1/A, Tel. 659 297

SACROFANO

All that remains of the medieval Jewish community is the street called "Ghetto Vecchio."

SEGNI

ANCIENT JEWISH QUARTER Via della Giudea

SERMONETA

ANCIENT SYNAGOGUE Via Marconi #15

The Jewish quarter extended from the Porta degli Annibaldi to the Palazza del Trivio. The ancient cemetery was on the street which leads to the Valvisciolo Abbey.

SEZZE

There is an ancient Jewish cemetery in this city.

VELLETRI

ANCIENT SYNAGOGUE Via della Stamperia

VITERBO

The Jewish community of Viterbo was noted for its poets, doctors, and rabbis. Some Jewish families still have the surname, Viterbo.

ANCIENT SYNAGOGUES Contrada San Biagio

There were two synagogues on this street in 1569.

GHETTO SITE Contrada de Valle Piatta

The Jews were expelled from this city at the end of the 16th century.

VITORCHIANO

HOUSE of the RABBI Via Ughelli #28

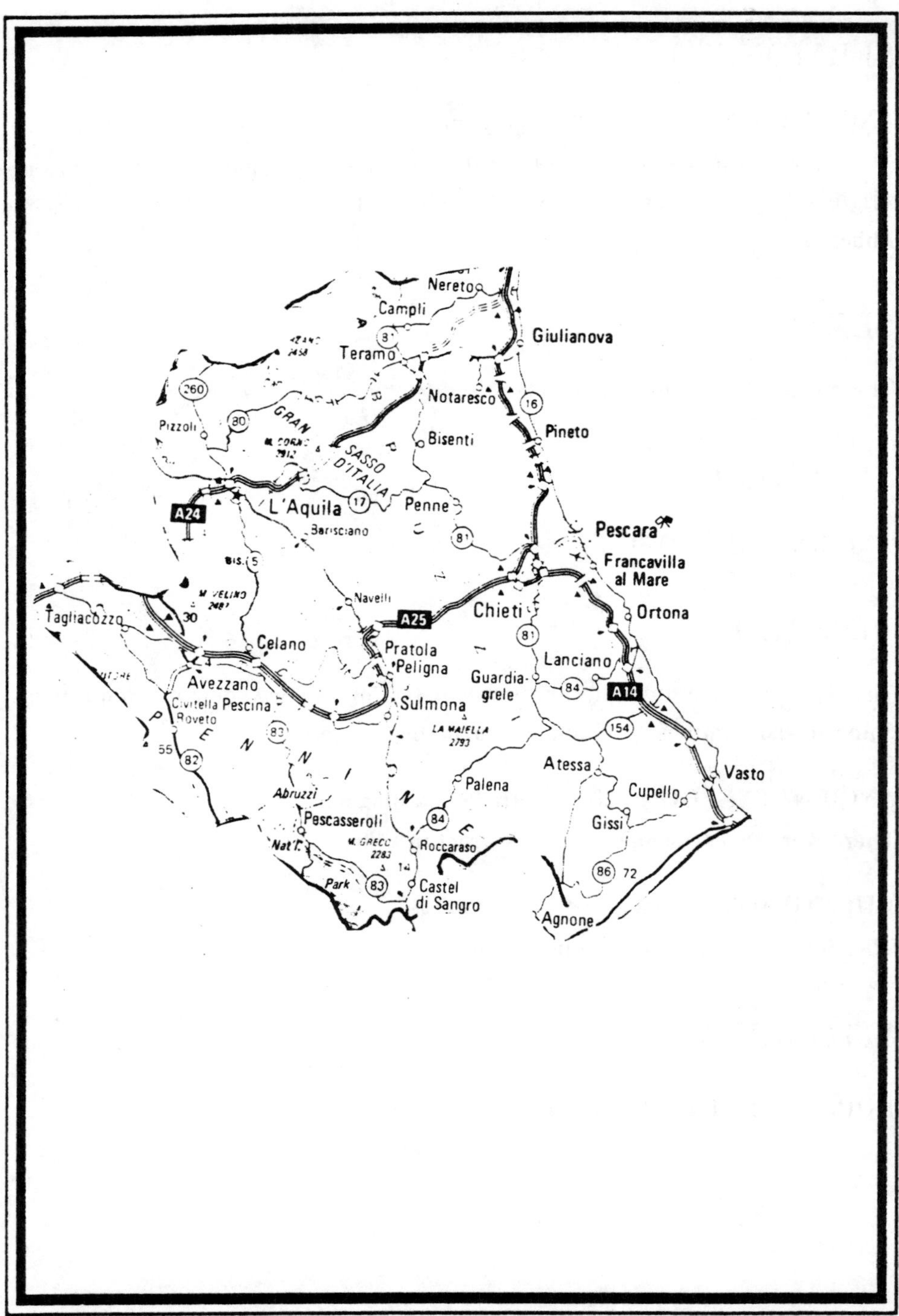

Nereto
Campli
Giulianova
Teramo
260
80
Notaresco
16
Pizzoli
GRAN
SASSO
D'ITALIA
Bisenti
Pineto
A24
L'Aquila
17
Penne
Pescara
Barisciano
81
Francavilla
al Mare
Navelli
Tagliacozzo
30
A25
Chieti
Ortona
Celano
Pratola
Peligna
81
Lanciano
Avezzano
Guardia-
grele
84
A14
Civitella
Roveto
Pescina
Sulmona
LA MAIELLA
2793
154
83
55
82
Atessa
Vasto
Palena
Cupello
Abruzzi
Pescasseroli
84
Gissi
Nat'l.
M. GRECO
2283
Roccaraso
14
Park
83
Castel
di Sangro
86
72
Agnone

Abruzzo Region

Benjamin of Tudela, in his "Book of Travels" (*Sefer ha-Masa'ot*), passed through Abruzzo and continued on to the Puglia region, which had a more active cultural life. The first Jews arrived in Aterno around the year 1062. There is a record of ten Jews who were killed in that city after being accused of desecrating the Host.

The Jews of Lanciano were expelled by Lord Roberto Bassavilla in 1156, when they sided with the Norman king, William the Conqueror. In the 1400s, there was a period of tranquility in the region. Jews received permission to trade in the cities of l'Aquila, Sulmona, Ortona, Cittaducale, and Guardiagrele. The second half of the 15th century was a period of continuous harassment. The Jews of Abruzzo were the first to abandon their homes, and choose exile. Some remained, but converted to Christianity. Jews returned to Lanciano in 1514, only to attend trade fairs.

L'AQUILA

This city was one of the greatest hotbeds of anti-Semitic intolerance in the 15th century. These intolerances were perpetrated by Giovanni da Capistrano, Jacopo da Monteprandone (1466), and Bernardino da Feltre (1488).

LANCIANO

ANCIENT JEWISH QUARTER

The history of the Jewish community is one of restrictions and expulsions. When they were permitted to return in 1191, the Jews were required to live in the *Quartiere della Scacca.* They remained on that enclosed street until the 16th century.

Lighting the Chanukah Menorah.

Sessa Aurunca
Piedimonte d'Alife
S. Bartolomeo in Galdo
Carinola
Pontelandolfo
Capua
Caserta
S. Maria Capua Vetere
Benevento
Maddaloni
Ariano Irpino
Aversa
Afragola
M. AVELLA 1591
Grottaminarda
NAPOLI
Nola
Baiano
Atripalda
Lacedonia
MT. VESUVIO 1277
Avellino
Ercolano
Pompei
Sarno
Lioni
Solofra
Montella
M. CERVIALTO 1809
Ravello
Salerno
Acerno
Laviano
Positano
Amalfi
M. MARZANO 1530
Capri
Eboli
Battipaglia
Serre
Controne
Paestum
Polla
Capaccio
Roccadaspide
Agropoli
Castellabate
Teggiano
M. CERVATI 1899
Pollica
Vallo della Lucania
Sanza
Ascea
MTE BULGHERA 1225
Lagonegro
Camerota
Sapri
A2
A30
A16
A3

Campania Region

There have been many Jewish centers scattered throughout the ports in the Gulf of Naples. Merchant centers thrived in Campania Felix and on the slopes of Mount Vesuvius. During the Roman period, there was a large Jewish community in Pozzuoli. They were involved in commerce and in the fabrication of glassware and purple dye. Various Jewish inscriptions have been found on the walls of Ercolana and Pompeii. Many objects and frescos of Jewish interest have been put on display in the National Museum in Naples. Naples is the only city in the Campania region which has a Jewish community.

NAPLES (Napoli)

The first Jewish group settled in Naples at the end of the 1st century. In 536, Jews helped the Goths fight against the Byzantine troops. When Benjamin of Tudela visited the city, there were 500 Jews in the area of San Marcellino. There was a synagogue, Hebrew school, and cemetery.

In 1280, the Dominican priests spread anti-Jewish doctrines. The synagogue on Via del Tempio was converted into the Catholic Church of Santa Maria della Purita. The atmosphere was more tolerable in 1492. Many Jewish exiles from Sicily, Sardinia, and Spain were permitted to take refuge in Naples.

This all changed in 1510. The first expulsions of Jews were initiated. The masses left, but 200 wealthy Jews paid 300 ducati and were therefore permitted to remain. In 1535, the price was raised to 10,000 ducati. In 1541, all of the Jews, even the wealthiest, had to leave the Kingdom of Naples. They did not officially return until 1831.

In 1831, a small group of Jews settled in the Maltese Cross Hotel (Albergo Croce di Malta). One of the rooms served as a synagogue. The rebirth of the Jewish community of Naples is linked to the Rothschild family. The Rothschild Bank offered the Bourbons (under Ferdinand) an enormous loan. Carl Rothschild was in charge of this transaction. He was noted for his religious conviction and was nicknamed "mezuzah" by his family. In 1827, he moved to Naples and opened the first Italian branch of the Rothschild Bank.

The bank quickly became the most important institution in the Kingdom. Carl purchased the most beautiful villa on the Riviera and affixed the "mezuzah" on its doorpost. When Carl's son, Adolf, left Naples in 1900, the villa was used as a synagogue by the Jewish community. That building, now called the Villa Pignatelli, was too large for the needs of the community. It was sold to the city, and is now used as a city museum.

In 1864, the community rented space on Via Cappella Vecchia. It was to become the main synagogue of Naples. The rent was paid by Baron Carl Rothschild, for five years. The first rabbi was Beniamino Artom, of Asti. In 1900, the Rothschilds left Naples. Adolf's children were all girls. At that time, women were not permitted to manage the bank. He died that same year, and left a legacy of 100,000 Lire for the maintenance of the Jewish hospital. Two beds in the hospital have always been reserved for whomever was in need, with a preference for Jews. These two beds still exist today. He also established a school for Jewish children.

During the last war, 14 Jews were deported by the Nazis. At the end of the war, there were 534 Jews living in Naples. Today, there are about 300.

ANCIENT SYNAGOGUE Via del Tempio #14

This former synagogue was converted into the Church of Santa Maria della Purita, in 1280.

SYNAGOGUE Vico Santa Maria a Cappella Vecchia #31 Tel. (081) 416 386

This synagogue follows the Spanish ritual.

NATIONAL MUSEUM of NAPLES

Some of the original frescos have been removed from the houses in Pompeii and are now on display in the National Museum of Naples. Some frescos depict the Judgment of King Solomon and the Story of Jonah. Several sculptures, including four gilded bronze statuettes, displaying Jewish and/or Eastern features, have been found in Pompeii.

NATO JEWISH COMMUNITY

A large part of the Jewish community in Naples consists of NATO troops. Many of them are from the United States. There is a small synagogue at Via Scarfoglio, in Agnano which serves these troops.

JEWISH CEMETERY

The oldest cemetery dates back to the 4th and 5th centuries. It was located near the Artillery Barracks, on Corso Malta. A 13th century cemetery was located in the Piazza del Mercato, near the old Church del Carmine. A more recent Jewish cemetery was located at Posillipo. Its land was donated by the Rothschilds. It was used until 1860. At that time, the cemetery at Poggioreale was instituted. There are about 800 tombs in the Poggioreale cemetery, which is now closed. The present Jewish cemetery is situated on Via Maria del Pianto.

POMPEII

There are several traces of Jewish existence in the ancient ruined City of Pompeii. There are fourteen Hebrew names inscribed on the walls of houses. Many Jews assimilated into the society and changed their names to Latin.

CRIPTOPORTICO HOUSE Region I, Section 6, Number 2

The name "Jeshua" was found on the walls of the salon.

GLADIATOR'S BARRACKS (Caserma dei Gladiatori)
Region V, Section 5, Number 3

There is graffiti, with the name Iesus, on the wall.

VIA dell 'ABBONDAZA Region I, Section 8, Number 7

On this street was the shop of a Jewish wine-maker, Felix Youdaikou. Four wine amphorae, with Greek phrases, and the Latin name, Youdaikou, were found in this store. Some say that "Youdaikou" refers to the store-owner. Others say that it refers to the origin of the wine.

VIA dell 'ABBONDAZA Region III, Section 4, Number 1

This was the house of a certain Zosimo. He scribbled a calendar of the market-days which took place in Pompeii, Nola, Nocera, Pozzuoli, Capua, and Rome on his wall. Many say that this suggests that he was a Jew. Some say that Zosimo and Vitale are Greek and Latin derivations of the Jewish name "Chaim," which means "life."

VIA della FORTUNA Region VI, Section 12, Number 5

Some scholars say that the names "Maria" and "Marta" are derivations of the Hebrew name *Miriam.* This house belonged to M. Terenzo Eudosso. It was transformed into a weaving workshop. Two of the workers were named Maria and Vesbius Tamudianus. Some say that the name "Tamudianus" is derived from the city called "Tamud," in Palestine.

CENTENARY Region IX, Section 8, Number 7

This was the house of A. Rustio Vero. There is mention of a servant "Marta," on the walls of the latrine. The remark is meant as an object of derision, in a trivial joke.

SALLUSTIO HOUSE Region IV, Section 2, Number 4

The Jewish name "Libanus" appears on the walls of this house. It also appears in the Villa of the Mysteries. Libanos was a manager of the most important hotels in Pompeii. It is said that he was a free Jew who came from

Palestine. His actual name was A. Cossius, which is derived from "Cush," a country near Ethiopia.

HOUSE #14 Region I, Section 11, Number 14

In the vestibule of this house is an inscription which says "Poinum Cherem." There are two five-pointed stars on either side of the phrase. Scholars have questioned whether the Latin characters refer to the Hebrew word which refers to an impure object or exile, or the Hebrew word which refers to a "vineyard." The word "Poinum" can refer to the Greek word for flock (of Israel). It can possibly mean "punishment." which would indicate that the phrase was hastily written - perhaps during the eruption of Mount Vesuvius in the year 79.

The five- and six-pointed star has been incorporated as decoration in ancient synagogues in Israel (Capernaum). The stars have also been described in esoteric and magical literature, as an amulet filled with special powers.

HOUSE #26 Region IX, Section 1, Number 26

There is an inscription depicting Sodom and Gomorra. Some say that this was a sad prophecy regarding Pompeii, whose customs and morals at the time of the eruption were particularly relaxed.

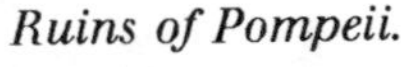

Ruins of Pompeii.

VICOLO del LUPANARE Region VII, Section 13, Numbers 11-14

This was a large two-story hotel which contained twenty-five beds. It was known as the "Hotel of the Jews."

Ercolano

HOUSE of LARARIO Section V, Number 31

There are several traces of a Jewish presence in these archaeological ruins. There is an inscription with the name "David" on one of the walls. The name "Abdeus Liviae" is found on some of the wall tiles. Scholars interpret this name as "Ovadia," the servant, or "Avda," the Hebrew word for servant.

Medieval Jewish scholar.

Sannicandro Garganico
Rodi
Garganico
Peschici
Apricena
San Severo
San Marco
in Lamis
Cagnano
Varano
GARGANO
DEL
Vieste
Monte
Sant' Angelo
PROMONTORIO
Mattinata
Lucera
Manfredonia
Fóggia
Golfo di
Manfredonia
A14
Bovino
Deliceto
Ascoli
Satriano
Orta
Nova
Margherita
di Savoia
Cerignola
A16
Barletta
Candela
Trani
Canosa
di Puglia
Andria
Bisceglie
Molfetta
Giovinazzo
Corato
Venosa
Spinazzola
Bitonto
Bari
Toritto
Mola di Bari
Gravina
di Puglia
Acquaviva
delle Fonti
Casamassima
Altamura
Polignano a Mare
Monopoli
Gioia
del Colle
Matera
Fasano
Alberobello
Laterza
Castellaneta
Montescaglioso
Martina
Franca
Villanova
Mottola
Massafra
Ostuni
Grottaglie
Ceglie
Messapico
Brindisi
Taranto
Oria
Francavilla
Fontana
Mesagne
Pulsano
Erchie
Manduria
Squinzano
Avetrana
Veglie
S. Cataldo
Leverano
Lecce
Nardo
Galatone
Galatina
Gallipoli
Maglie
Otra
Casarano
Ugento
Tricase
Leuca
CAPO S. MARIA
San Cesarea Terme

Puglia Region

In Roman times, the major trade route from the Middle East to Rome was along the Appian Way, from the Ports of Bari and Brindisi. There were many small Jewish communities along this route. After fifteen centuries of an uninterrupted settlement, the Jewish communities were wiped out in a relatively short period of time. There are few traces of these early communities.

Medieval Italian Jews.

CASTELLANETA

ANCIENT JEWISH QUARTER Via Giudea

ORIA

RIONE GIUDEA (Jewish District) Porta degli ebrei

There is a *Menorah* at the entrance to the present Jewish District, which is located on the site of the old Jewish quarter. The Jewish community of Oria descended from Jewish prisoners who were brought as slaves from Jerusalem by Emperor Titus.

There was a renowned Academy of Jewish Studies in this city during the Middle Ages. Some of the noted scholars included Shabbatai ben Abraham Donnolo, who was a pharmacologist, doctor and scientist of the 10th century, and the poet, Achimaaz.

SAN CESAREA TERME

During World War II, Jewish soldiers from the Palestine Brigade of the Allied 8th Armada stopped in this city before advancing up the Italian peninsula with the Allied Forces. There is a sign, printed in Hebrew, documenting this event.

ANCIENT JEWISH COMMUNITIES

The following cities hosted Jewish communities:

Acri, Altomonto, Arena, Belcastro, Bisignano, Carpanzano, Cassano, Castelvetere, Celico, Castrovillari, Corigliano, Cosenza, Crotone, Galatro, Gerace, Grimaldi, Lattarico, Magli, Martirano, Mesoraca, Montafollone, Montalto, Morano, Nicastro, Nicotera, Paterno, Reggio Calabria, Rende, Rogliano, Rossano, San Marco d'Alunzio, San Severina, Scogliano, Seminara, Simeri, Squillace, Strongoli, Taverna, Tritani, Tropea and Vaccarizzo

SANNICANDRO GARGANICO

In 1930, Donato Manduzio, a Christian, studied the Torah and all of its laws and interpretations. He attracted several followers in his town. Manduzio wanted to convert to Judaism, along with his fellow townspeople. The rabbinic authorities granted the conversions in 1944. After the conversions, many of his followers moved to Israel and applied the instructions of the Torah in the Holy Land. Their leader, Donato Manduzio, however, died in Sannicandro in 1948, before he was able to make the "aliyah."

TRANI

ANCIENT JEWISH QUARTER Via Giudea

There were 200 Jews living in Trani in the 12th century when Benjamin of Tudela visited the city. The community grew with crypto-Jews who fled from southern Spain after the Moors invaded. The region was ruled by the Normans, under Frederik II. He demonstrated particular benevolence with the Jewish communities. He gave the Jews fiscal control of their quarters and permitted them to maintain the monpoly of the silk trade and cloth dyeing.

The Dominican friars promoted a violent conversion campaign in the end of the 13th century. The fiscal control over the Jewish communities was returned to the bishops. The Jews had to wear identification marks on their clothing.

The Anjou monarchy was replaced by the Aragon family in 1442. The Jews were granted amnesty and the wearing of the identification markings was abolished. Nevertheless, there were many violent episodes against the Jews in Lecce, Brindisi and Trani.

King Ferdinand of Spain received the regions of Puglia and Calabria as a result of a partitioning of the lands in the Kingdom of Naples in 1505. The Jews were expelled from his territories. Some Jews remained and converted (in public) to Christianity. In private, however, they retained their Jewish identities and religious practices.

The gifted philosopher, Isaac ben Judah Abrabanel (1437-1508), was part of this exodus. His first flight was from Spain. He then became the economic consultant to King Ferrante of Naples and later to King Alphonse of Aragon. He lived in Monopoli prior to the expulsion. He then moved to Venice, where he also held prestigious positions.

SCOLANOVA CHURCH Via Sinagogo

This church was originally built as a synagogue.

CHURCH of SANTA ANNA

This church was built on the remains of an ancient synagogue. It is located in the old Jewish quarter.

VENOSA

CATACOMBS

There are two Jewish catacombs in Venosa. The oldest dates back to the 4th through 7th centuries. The second dates from the 9th century. These catacombs are not open to the public. There were Jewish settlements in Lavello, Matera and Melfi.

Illuminated marriage contract (Ketuba) from Livorno (1728), now housed in the Italian Synagogue in Jerusalem.

אשת חיל עטרת בעלה
בסימנא טבא ובמזלא מעליא

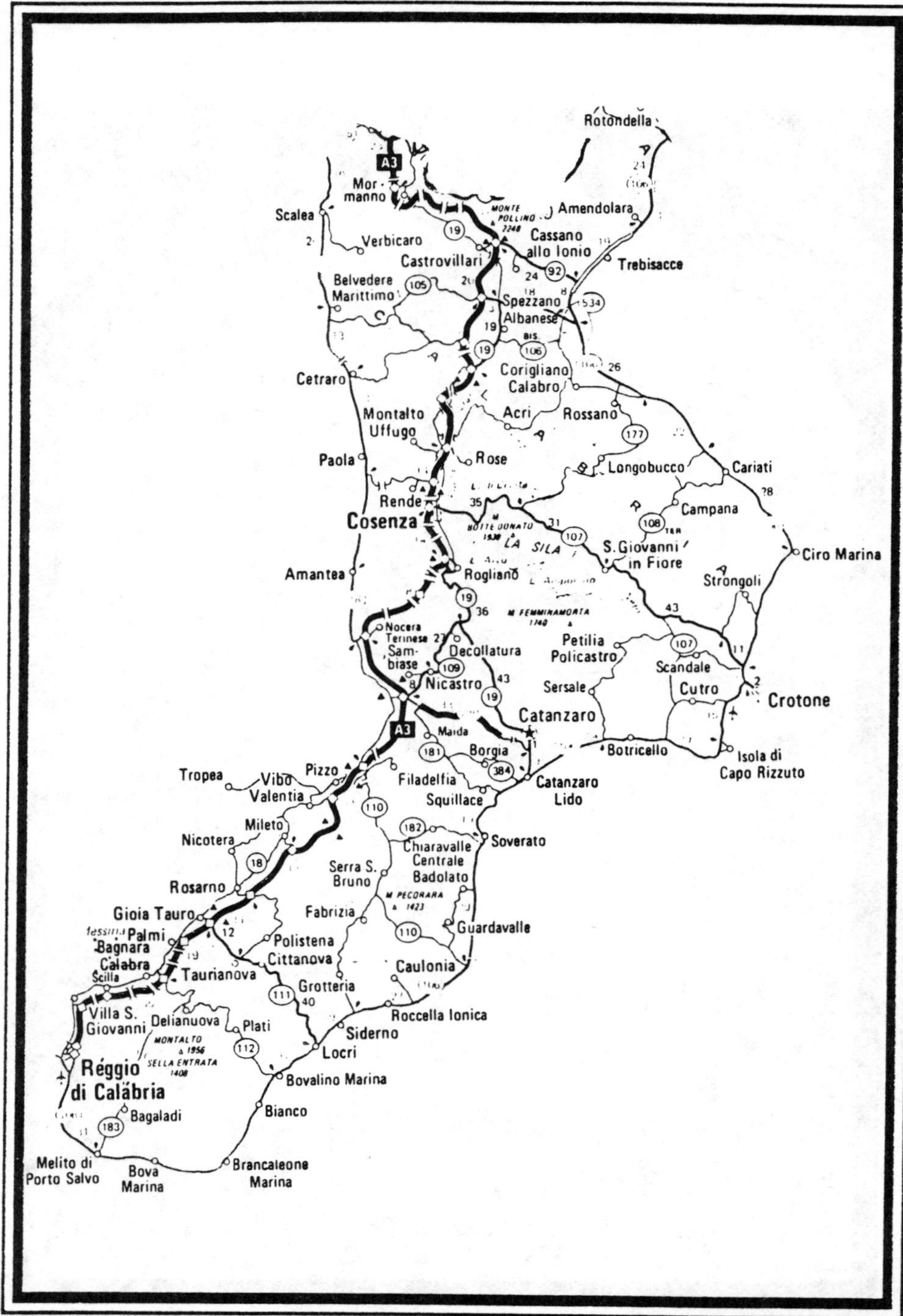

Rotondella
A3
Mormanno
Scalea
Monte Pollino 2248
Amendolara
Verbicaro
Cassano allo Ionio
Castrovillari
Trebisacce
Belvedere Marittimo
Spezzano Albanese
Cetraro
Corigliano Calabro
Montalto Uffugo
Acri
Rossano
Paola
Rose
Longobucco
Cariati
Rende
Campana
Cosenza
M. Botte Donato 1930
La Sila
S. Giovanni in Fiore
Ciro Marina
Amantea
Rogliano
Strongoli
M. Femminamorta 1740
Nocera Terinese
Sambiase
Decollatura
Petilia Policastro
Scandale
Nicastro
Sersale
Cutro
Crotone
Catanzaro
Maida
Borgia
Botricello
Isola di Capo Rizzuto
Tropea
Vibo Valentia
Pizzo
Filadelfia
Squillace
Catanzaro Lido
Mileto
Nicotera
Soverato
Chiaravalle Centrale
Badolato
Serra S. Bruno
Rosarno
M. Pecorara 1423
Gioia Tauro
Fabrizia
Guardavalle
Palmi
Polistena
Bagnara Calabra
Cittanova
Caulonia
Scilla
Taurianova
Grotteria
Villa S. Giovanni
Delianuova
Platì
Roccella Ionica
Siderno
Montalto 1956
Sella Entrata 1408
Locri
Réggio di Calàbria
Bovalino Marina
Bianco
Bagaladi
Melito di Porto Salvo
Bova Marina
Brancaleone Marina

Calabria Region

BOVA MARINA

During construction work on Highway SS 106, which links Catanzaro with Reggio Calabria, an ancient Roman town was discovered. The archaeological dig in 1986 uncovered a 2nd century synagogue. It is among the oldest synagogue ruins in Italy, along with that of Ostia Antica, near Rome.

The ruins consist of two buildings. One served as a vestibule, while the other served as the main sanctuary. The floor area is covered with mosaic tiles and marble "crustae." The mosaics display a design of floral crowns and the geometric motif of the so-called "Seal of Solomon." At one location, there is a mosaic design portraying a seven-branched *Menorah* and a *Lulav.*

CASTROVILLARI

This city was a major center for paper production. The ruins of an old paper mill, *Cartiera*, are found along the Lagano River. The synagogue was called "Muscita" by the locals. This clearly demonstrates the strong Arabic influence since the Arabic word for synagogue is *Moshea.*

CATANZARO

ANCIENT JEWISH QUARTER Via Capuana

The Jews were granted permission to trade in Textiles. In 1147, they introduced the cultivation of mulberries. They also worked in the silk industries.

COSENZA

ANCIENT JEWISH QUARTER

The old Jewish quarter, Giudecca, was located near the Vergini Monastery. In 1212, Frederic II granted the Jews permission to open a dyeworks. The city later became renowned for its silk industries. The practice of medicine also flourished among the Jews. In the 1430s, there were many Jewish surgeons such as Giuseppe Ebreo di Montalto, "Maestro" Nicolo Pagano and even a female Jewish physician, Cusina di Filippo de Pastino. She was granted permission to perform surgery on women.

The order to vacate the city was issued many times during the early 16th century. It was postponed several times as well. However, on October 31, 1541, all Jews were permanently expelled from Cosenza.

PIZZO

PASSO delle JUDIO (The Jew's Pass)

This was one of three passes between Serralta San Vito and San Vito Ionio.

REGGIO CALABRIA

Jews lived in the Jewish Quarter, Giudecca, and were involved in commerce. At the end of the 15th century, the entire Jewish community of Syracuse (Sicily) moved to Reggio Calabria. They introduced the use of indigo in the dyeing of cloth. In 1539, the Jews were expelled from this city.

ROSSANO

Following the Spanish Inquisition in 1492, the Jewish population in Italy increased by 40,000 to 50,000. Sixteen thousand Jews lived in Rossano during that period. There were still 6,000 Jews in 1532, between the expulsions of 1510 and 1539. Today, there are no Jews living in Rossano.

Sabbath kiddush.

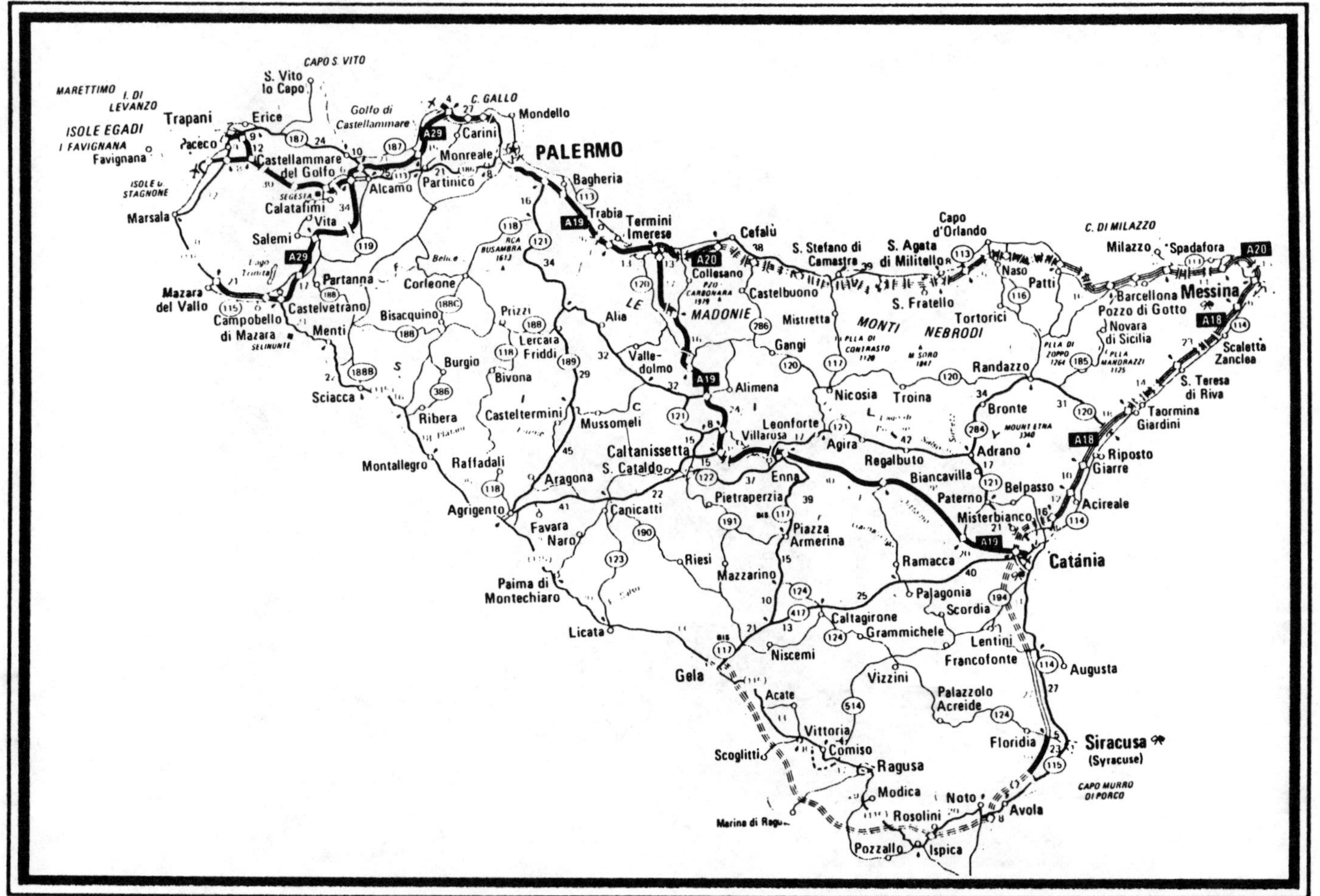

CAPO S. VITO
S. Vito lo Capo
MARETTIMO
I. DI LEVANZO
ISOLE EGADI
I. FAVIGNANA
Favignana
Trapani
Erice
Paceco
Golfo di Castellammare
C. GALLO
Mondello
PALERMO
Carini
Monreale
Partinico
Castellammare del Golfo
Alcamo
SEGESTA
Calatafimi
Vita
Salemi
ISOLE d. STAGNONE
Marsala
Mazara del Vallo
Campobello di Mazara
SELINUNTE
Castelvetrano
Partanna
Menti
Sciacca
Corleone
Bisacquino
Burgio
Ribera
Montallegro
Raffadali
Agrigento
Prizzi
Lercara Friddi
Bivona
Casteltermini
RCA BUSAMBRA 1613
Bagheria
Trabia
Termini Imerese
Alia
Valledolmo
Mussomeli
Aragona
Favara
Naro
Palma di Montechiaro
Licata
Canicatti
S. Cataldo
Caltanissetta
Cefalù
Collesano
PZO CARBONARA 1979
Castelbuono
LE MADONIE
Gangi
Alimena
Villarusa
Enna
Pietraperzia
Piazza Armerina
Riesi
Mazzarino
Gela
Niscemi
S. Stefano di Camastra
Mistretta
Nicosia
Leonforte
Agira
PLLA DI CONTRASTO 1120
MONTI NEBRODI
M. SORO 1847
S. Agata di Militello
Capo d'Orlando
S. Fratello
Tortorici
Troina
Regalbuto
Naso
Patti
Randazzo
Bronte
MOUNT ETNA 3340
Adrano
Biancavilla
Paterno
Belpasso
Misterbianco
Catánia
Acireale
Giarre
Riposto
C. DI MILAZZO
Milazzo
Spadafora
Messina
Barcellona Pozzo di Gotto
Novara di Sicilia
PLLA DI ZOPPO 1264
PLLA MANDRAZZI 1125
Scaletta Zanclea
S. Teresa di Riva
Taormina Giardini
Ramacca
Palagonia
Scordia
Caltagirone
Grammichele
Lentini
Francofonte
Augusta
Vizzini
Palazzolo Acreide
Floridia
Siracusa
(Syracuse)
CAPO MURRO DI PORCO
Acate
Vittoria
Comiso
Scoglitti
Ragusa
Modica
Noto
Avola
Rosolini
Pozzallo
Ispica
Marina di Ragusa
A19
A20
A29
A18

Sicily Region

Sicily was the most important Jewish settlement in southern Italy before 1492. Its population was 100,000 and was divided into fifty-two communities. The Jewish population in the entire Italy, today, numbers less than half of the Jewish population in Sicily at the end of the 15th century.

The first Jewish settlement dates back to before the destruction of the Temple in Jerusalem. Its ports attracted many merchants who had contacts with other countries throughout the Mediterranean. In 590, Pope Gregory ordered the ecclesiastical authorities to restitute all of the property which was taken from the Jews during the period of anti-Jewish oppression and forced conversions. This included the spoils gained from the expropriations of the synagogues.

Some Jews arrived in Palermo as prisoners of the Arabs. Under the rule of the Arabs, the Jews still enjoyed a fair amount of liberty. When the Normans arrived in southern Italy, the Sicilian Jews received privileges from King Ruggero I in 1094. Benjamin of Tudela refers to the Jewish communities of Messina and Palermo.

Restrictions against the Jews started again in 1296. Jewish doctors were not permitted to treat Christians. They were prohibited from holding public office nor could they employ Christian servants. Synagogues were not permitted to have any exterior decorations. In Syracuse, however, they were permitted to build a synagogue. Jews were required to wear the identification mark.

In 1392, Martin of Aragon ascended to the throne, during a period of massacres and violent anti-Jewish persecutions. The end of the 15th century witnessed a period of new persecutions, which took the pretext of the profanation of the Host by the Jews, and the so-called ritual murders. On the day before Christmas of 1491, a stone broke the cross which was being carried in the processional in Castiglione. The rabbi of the city was held responsible for the action and was publically executed.

On March 31, 1492, King Ferdinand the Catholic issued the Decree of Expulsion. The Jews had three months in order to settle their affairs and debts and leave the island. The final deadline was extended to December 31, 1492.

After the majority of the Jewish population left Sicily, the synagogues were converted into churches. The cemeteries were desecrated. Some Jews remained in Sicily after they publically converted to Christianity. In private, however, they retained their Jewish identity and customs. These were the secret Jews or *marranos*. The Jews moved to Puglia, Calabria, and Naples. Many moved to other regions in the Mediterranean basin such as Istanbul, Damascus, Salonika, and Cairo.

The Sicilian Jews were involved in business and moneylending. They were also involved in agriculture, especially, in the cultivation of date palms and vineyards. The synagogue was often called *meskita,* which is a derivation from the Arab term *moschea.* In Palermo, there was a Vicolo Meschitta. The rabbis were called *dienchehila,* which is derived from the Hebrew *dayan kehillah.*

These were some of the Jewish settlements in Sicily before the expulsion: Adrano, Agrigento, Alcamo, Alcara, Augusta, Bivona, Caccamo, Calascibetta, Caltabellotta, Caltagirone, Caltanissetta, Cammarata, Castiglione, Castrgiovanni, Castronuouva, Castroreale, Catania, Cefalu, Ciminna, Corleone, Gerace, Giuliana, Lentini, Licata, Marsala, Mazara del Vallo, Messina, Milazzo, Militello, Mineo, Modica, Monte San Giuliano, Naro, Nicosia, Noto, Palazzolo, Palermo, Paterno, Piana degli Albanesi, Piazza Armerina, Polizzi, Ragusa, Randazza, Regalbuto, Salemi, Santa Lucia, San Marco, Savoca, Scacca, Scicli, Syracuse, Taormina, Termini, Imerese, Trapani, Vicari, and Vizzini.

In 1740, the Jews were invited back to Sicily. Few accepted the invitation, and no Jewish community existed until the last century.

AGIRA

ANCIENT SYNAGOGUE

The Church of San Croce was originally built as a synagogue.

CATANIA

ANCIENT SYNAGOGUES

There were two Jewish sections in this city. The upper Jewish quarter was located within the old walls, between degli Infanti Bastion, del Tindaro Bastion, San Giovanni and San Euplio Bastions. The synagogue was located near the Church of San Giovanni. Adjoining the synagogue was the Jewish hospital. A smaller synagogue was located in the lower portion of the city center.

ANCIENT JEWISH CEMETERY

The Jewish cemetery was located outside the Porta del Tonnaro, in Santa Maria della Catena. It was submerged in a lava flow during the eruption of Mount Etna in 1669.

ERICE

A. CORDICI MUSEUM

This museum contains records of the ancient synagogue in the city.

MESSINA

ANCIENT JEWISH QUARTER

In 1347, the Jews were condemned to death after they were found guilty of ritual murder. This event is recorded on a stone tablet located on the façade of the Cathedral of Messina.

The old Jewish quarter was situated in the Paraporto section, near the Church of San Filippo. The *Porta Giudea*, or Jewish portal, was nearby. Messina was noted for its many Jewish doctors. There were an estimated 2,400 Jews living in Messina in 1492. There were many synagogues in the city, however, there are no remnants of any of these houses of worship.

NOTO

JEWISH CATACOMB

The Jewish catacomb is located east of the Flaccavento House. The catacombs contain etchings of two *Menoras.*

PALERMO

ANCIENT JEWISH QUARTER

In 1312, the Jews were forced to live outside the walls of the city. The synagogue was located near the Church of San Nicolo da Tolentino. Before this eviction, the Jews lived in the old city, in the Cassero section, near Corso Vittorio Emanuel.

Many Jews were fisherman, while others had the monopoly on the silk industry. In 1492, 5,000 Jews were expelled from Palermo.

SCICLI

ANCIENT SYNAGOGUE

There were two synagogues in this city. One was known as the "rocky" synagogue, since it was located in a grotto. It was used in 1461 and was located near the Modica Port.

SYRACUSE

The Jewish community of Syracuse was second only to that of Palermo. The Jewish quarter was located in the Acradina section. Many artifacts such as an oil lamp and sepulchral hypogea, are on display in the National Museum of Syracuse.

TAORMINA

At the time of the expulsion in 1492, the Jews of Taormina were given permission by the Viceroy to take along only one blanket per family. They were also permitted to take along some cheese for their journey.

TRAPANI

ANCIENT SYNAGOGUE

The Jewish quarter was located in the San Pietro area. It was on the Via Biscottai and Via San Pietro. The synagogue was called "Moshea." There was also a Superior School of Judaic Studies. The Palazza della Giudecca was located in this section.

Ancient synagogue of Trapani.

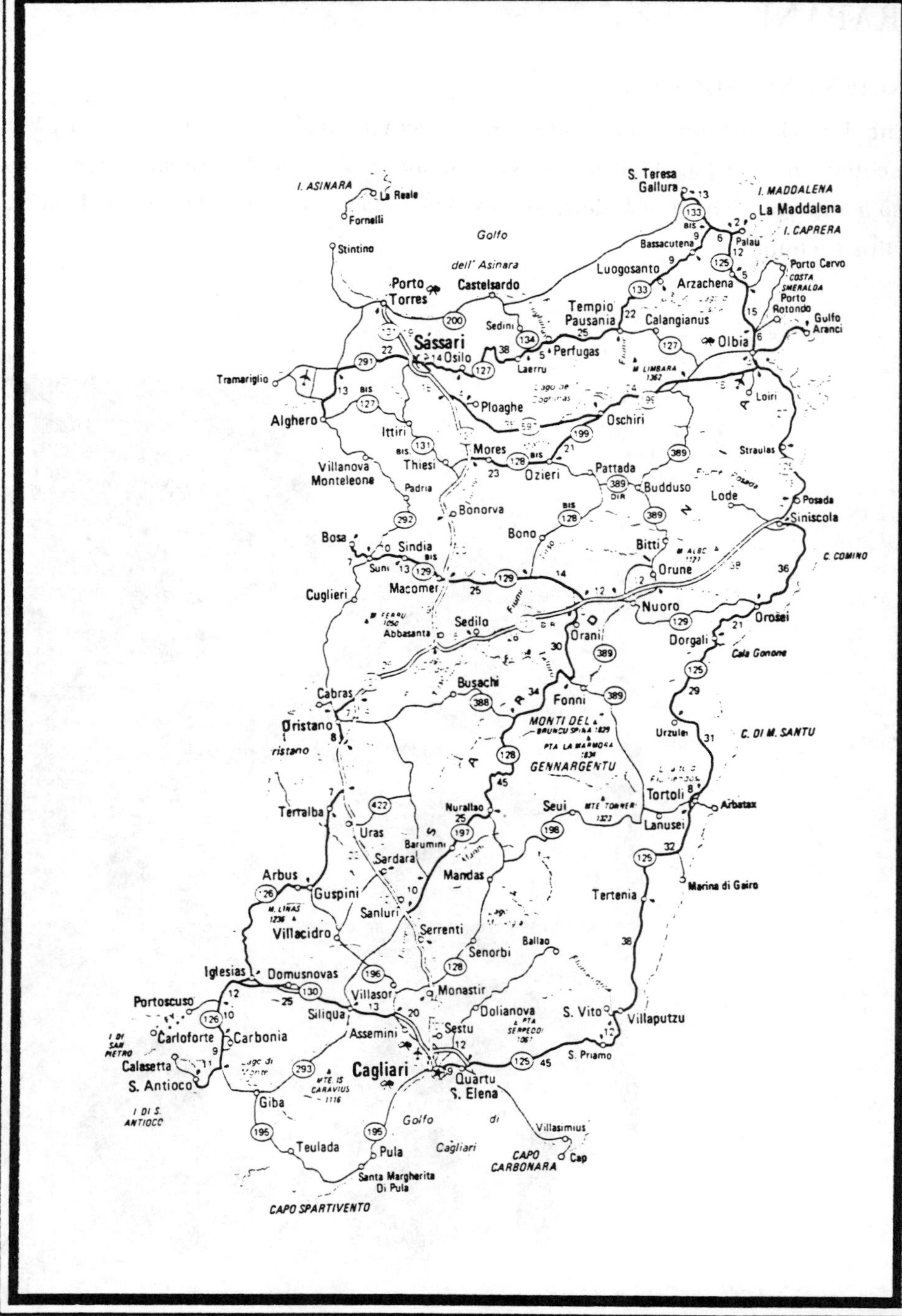
I. ASINARA
La Reale
Fornelli
Stintino
Golfo
dell' Asinara
Porto Torres
Castelsardo
Sassari
Osilo
Sedini
Perfugas
Laerru
Tramariglio
Alghero
Ploaghe
Ittiri
Thiesi
Mores
Ozieri
Oschiri
Villanova Monteleone
Padria
Bonorva
Bosa
Sindia
Suni
Macomer
Cuglieri
Abbasanta
Sedilo
Cabras
Busachi
Oristano
Terralba
Uras
Sardara
Barumini
Nurallao
Arbus
Guspini
Sanluri
Mandas
Villacidro
Serrenti
Senorbi
Ballao
Iglesias
Domusnovas
Villasor
Monastir
Portoscuso
Siliqua
Dolianova
Carloforte
Carbonia
Assemini
Sestu
Calasetta
S. Antioco
Cagliari
Quartu
S. Elena
Giba
Teulada
Pula
Santa Margherita Di Pula
CAPO SPARTIVENTO
Golfo di Cagliari
Villasimius
CAPO CARBONARA
Cap
S. Teresa Gallura
I. MADDALENA
La Maddalena
I. CAPRERA
Palau
Bassacutena
Luogosanto
Arzachena
Porto Cervo
COSTA SMERALDA
Porto Rotondo
Golfo Aranci
Tempio Pausania
Calangianus
Olbia
M. LIMBARA 1362
Loiri
Straulas
Pattada
Budduso
Lode
Posada
Siniscola
Bono
Bitti
Orune
C. COMINO
Nuoro
Orosei
Orani
Dorgali
Cala Gonone
Fonni
MONTI DEL GENNARGENTU
Urzulei
C. DI M. SANTU
Tortoli
Arbatax
Seui
Lanusei
Marina di Gairo
Tertenia
S. Vito
Villaputzu
S. Priamo
MTE IS CARAVIUS 1116

Sardinia Region

The Jewish presence on the island during the Roman period is testimonialized by the discovery of catacombs in Sant 'Antioch. During the Middle Ages, until the arrival of the House of Aragon in 1326, the conditions of the Jews was generally good. In 1430, their condition began to worsen. The Jews had to wear the identification mark, were not allowed to wear jewelry, and were only permitted to wear black shoes. They were not permitted to work on Christian Holy Days and could not travel into the interior of the island for commercial endeavors. The Jews were forced into a ghetto.

On July 31, 1492, a large group of Jews left from the Port of Cagliari. Many died during the arduous journey. All of their wealth was confiscated at the port. Some Jews converted to Christianity. Only then, were they permitted to remain and continue their trades. The synagogue of Cagliari and Alghero were transformed into churches. The Jews fled to the Kingdom of Naples, North Africa, and Turkey. The surname, Sardinia, was used by many Jews in Istanbul following the expulsion.

ALGHERO

TOWERS of the JEWS (Torre degli ebrei)

These towers were financed by the Jewish community of Cagliari and built by local Jews in 1360. There is an historic plaque which records this event. There was a synagogue which was built in 1381 and enlarged in 1438. The cemetery dates back to 1383. In 1390, the gifted doctor and Talmudist, Yehudah ben David (a.k.a. Nonjusas Bondavin), became the rabbi over all the Jews in Sardinia.

The riches and influence of the Jews grew considerably in the 15th century. In 1459, Zare Carcassona financed the Royal galley. Other members of that family accumulated great wealth and property. They owned all of the houses in the Jewish quarter.

Thus, when the Jews were ordered either to convert to Christianity or leave the island, the Carcassonas preferred conversion. They remained in Sardinia, with their power and prestige, as Christians.

CAGLIARI

ANCIENT SYNAGOGUE Via del Guidei

The Church of San Croce was originally designed as a synagogue. Cagliari was the largest Jewish settlement on the island. They lived near the port and were merchants, peddlers, moneychangers and usurers. Several Jews were physicians.

In 1459, Abramo di Capro wrote a book about the medicinal herbs of Sardinia. The poorer Jews dealt in old iron scraps and pins. Some were involved with furs and textiles, while others produced fabrics or exported cheese.

IGLESIAS

The Jews in this city were involved in mining ore.

PANTELERRIA

There were 1,000 Jews on this island north of Sicily in 1200. They lived inside the castle. Pantelerria was under the same jurisdiction as Sicily.

Tower of the Jews.

SANT 'ANTIOCO

There are Jewish catacombs dating from the 4th and 5th centuries in this city.

BIBLIOGRAPHY

Encyclopaedia judaica, 16 voll., Keter, Jerusalem 1971, con quattro supplementi: *Year Book* 1973, 1974, 1975-76 e *Decennial Book* 1973-82 (in inglese).
J. Maier - P. Schäfer, *Piccola enciclopedia dell'ebraismo*, Marietti, Casale Monferrato 1985.
A. Milano, *Storia degli ebrei in Italia*, Einaudi, Torino 1963.
Italia judaica. Atti del I Convegno internazionale, Bari 18-22 maggio 1981, Archivi di Stato, Roma 1983.
«*Italia. Studi e ricerche sulla cultura e sul'la letteratura degli ebrei d'Italia*», 1976 - (edito dall'Università ebraica di Gerusalemme).
«*Rassegna mensile di Israel*», Roma 1925 - D'ora in avanti citata come in RMI.

Piedmont Region

Aa.Vv., *Ebrei a Torino, Ricerche per il centenario della sinagoga (1884-1984)*, Allemandi, Torino 1984.
Aa.Vv., *La sinagoga di Casale Monferrato. Cenni storico-illustrativi*, comunità israelitica di Casale, Casale 1969.
Aa.Vv., *Gli ebrei di Asti. Momenti di vita ebraica: raccolta di articoli e documenti*, Asti 1980 (cicl.).
Aa.Vv., *Gli ebrei nell'astigiano. Testimonianze e indagini*, Asti 1982.
Aa.Vv., *Insediamento ebraico in Asti*, Assessorato alla cultura della Regione Piemonte in collaborazione con l'Archivio Terracini, Torino 1984.
Aa.Vv., *Insediamento ebraico a Biella*, Assessorato... ivi 1984.
Aa.Vv., *Insediamento ebraico a Cherasco*, Assessorato... ivi 1984.
Aa.Vv., *Insediamento ebraico a Chieri*, Assessorato... ivi 1983.
Aa.Vv., *Insediamento ebraico a Torino*, Assessorato... ivi 1984.
M.D. Anfossi, *Gli ebrei in Piemonte. Loro condizioni guridico-sociali dal 1430 all'emancipazione*, Anfossi e C., Torino 1914.
G. Arian Levi, *Gli ebrei in Piemonte nell'ultimo decennio del sec. XVIII*, in RMI, 9 (1935), 10-12, 511-534.
Id., *Sulle premesse social-economiche dell'emancipazione degli ebrei nel Regno di Sardegna (In base a documenti del periodo 1814-40)*, in RMI, 18 (1952), 10, 412-437.
Id., *Vita quotidiana nel ghetto di Torino sulla fine dell'800*, in RMI, 45 (1979), 6-7, 255-265.
R. Arnaldi, *Immagini di un passato ebraico nel Monregalese, I quaderni de «La Ghisleriana»*, 2, Mondovì 1982.
G. Artom, *I giorni del mondo*, Longanesi, Milano 1981.
G. Avigdor, *La sinagoga di Casale*, in Aa.Vv., *Atti del quarto congresso di antichità e d'arte*, 1969.
C. Bertola, *Vita e cultura ebraica. Documentazione fotografica sulla presenza ebraica in Piemonte nei secoli XVIII e XIX a cura di Giorgio Avigdor*, Torino 1983.
A.S. Bessone - M. Vercellotti, *Il piazzo di Biella*, P.R., Biella 1976.
D. Colombo, *Alcuni appunti sul ghetto di Vercelli*, in RMI, 42 (1976), 7-8, 374-377.

ID., *Il Ghetto di Acqui*, in RMI, 41 (1975), 7-8, 361-379.
ID., *Il Ghetto di Biella*, in RMI, 43 (1977), 11-12, 672-677.
ID., *Il Ghetto di Mondovì*, in RMI, 34 (1968), 4, 233-237.
ID., *Il Ghetto di Nizza Monferrato*, in RMI, 40 (1974), 1, 52-56 .
ID., *Il Ghetto di Savigliano*, in RMI, 39 (1973), 1, 58-61.
ID., *Il Ghetto di Torino e il suo antico cimitero*, in RMI, 41 (1975), 5-6, 311-317.
ID., *Trino vercellese e le sue tipografie ebraiche*, in RMI, 37 (1971), 11, 723-724.
ID., *Ivrea ebraica*, in «Ha keillah», 5 (1979), 1, 3.
D. COLOMBO - G. TEDESCO, *Il Ghetto di Carmagnola*, in RMI, 27 (1961), 12, 536-549.
ID., *Il Ghetto di Chieri*, in RMI, 27 (1961), 2, 63-66; 4, 172-178.
ID., *Il Ghetto di Fossano*, in RMI, 29 (1963), 3-4, 129-141.
E. DE BENEDETTI, *Gli ebrei a Cherasco*, in RMI, 21 (1955), 11, 461-465.
P. DE BENEDETTI, *Ancora sugli ebrei di Asti*, in «Il Platano», 4 (1979), 5,43-46.
ID., *Gli ebrei di Asti e il loro rito*, in «Il Platano», 2 (1977), 4, 17-28.
ID., *Una poesia sul ghetto di Moncalvo*, in «Il Platano», 3 (1978), 6, 10-16.
N. DIENA, *Sei documenti (e cinque fotografie) sugli ebrei di Carmagnola*, in RMI, 25 (1959), 8-9, 363-366.
D. DISEGNI, *Il rito di Asti-Fossano-Moncalvo (Appam)*, in U. Nahon (a c. di), *Scritti in onore di Sally Mayer*, Fondazione Sally Mayer, Milano-Gerusalemme 1956, 78-81.
A. DRAGONE, *Il tempietto ebraico di Carmagnola*, in «Cronache di Palazzo Cisterna», 1967, 3.
S. FOA, *Banchi e banchieri nel Piemonte nei secoli scorsi*, in RMI, 21 (1955), 1-2, 38-50; 3, 85-97; 4, 127-136; 5, 190-201; 7, 284-297; 8, 325-326; 11, 471-485.
ID., *Cronache ebraiche-torinesi del primo '700*, in RMI, 15 (1949), 11-12, 529-537.
ID., *Gli ebrei in Alessandria*, RMI, Città di Castello 1959.
ID., *Gli ebrei nel Monferrato nei secoli XVI e XVII*, Forni, Bologna 1965 (rist. anast.).
ID., *L'istituzione del Ghetto in Acqui*, in RMI, 19 (1953), 4, 163-174; 5, 206-217.
ID., *L'istituzione del Ghetto a Moncalvo* (1732), in AA.VV., *Scritti in onore di Riccardo Bachi*, in RMI, 16 (1950), 6-8, 188-201.
ID., *Vicende del ghetto di Torino*, «Bollettino della comunità israelitica di Milano», Milano 1963.
R. GREMM, *Gli ebrei in Piemonte. Moncalvo*, «Bollettino della comunità israelitica di Milano», 36 (1978).
A.C. JEMOLO, *Gli ebrei piemontesi e il ghetto intorno al 1835-40*, Accademia delle scienze di Torino, Torino 1952.
E. LOEWENTHAL, *Vita ebraica a Torino fra l'800 e il '900*, in «Studi piemontesi», 14 (1985), 1, 117-123.
A. MILANO, *Immagini del passato ebraico, Comunità Piemontesi*, RMI, Roma 1974.
S. OLIVETTI, *La comunità israelitica di Chieri*, in RMI, 24 (1958), 7, 317-319.
N. PAVONCELLO, *La tipografia ebraica in Piemonte*, in RMI, 34 (1970), 2, 96-100.
M. PELLEGRINI, *Le aree segregate: approcci teorici e un caso storico. Il ghetto di Torino*, Celid, Torino 1979.
T. SARASSO, *Storia degli ebrei a Vercelli*, Comunità israelitica, Vercelli 1974.
A. SEGRE, *Memorie di vita ebraica. Casale Monferrato, Roma, Gerusalemme. 1918-1960*, Bonacci, Roma 1979.

V. Segre, *Cenni storici sulla comunità di Saluzzo*, in RMI, 37 (1971), 8, 500-513.
S. Taricco, *La sinagoga di Asti*, in «Il Platano», 2 (1977), 4, 29-32.
S. Treves, *Gli ebrei a Chieri (1416-1418)*, Cronache chieresi, Chieri 1974.
L. Voghera Luzzatto, *Emancipazione ebraica ad Asti*, in «Il Platano», 5 (1980), 2, 92-102.
Id., *Una finestra sul ghetto. Stefano Incisa e gli ebrei di Asti*, Carucci, Roma 1983.
Id. (a c. di), *Documenti per la storia del ghetto di Asti*, Asti 1981 (fasc. ciclost.).

Liguria Region

C. Brizzolari, *Gli ebrei nella storia di Genova*, Sabatelli, Genova 1971.
A. Croccolo, *Appunti sulla comunità israelitica della nostra città*, «Il Telegrafo» (cronaca di La Spezia), Livorno 2-12-1964.
Dizionario delle strade di Genova, I, Genova 1967.
G. Fiaschini, *Ebrei a Savona nel '400*, in Aa.Vv., *Savona nel Quattrocento e l'istituzione del Monte di Pietà*, Cassa di Risparmio di Savona, Savona 1980, 199-206.
A. Luzzatto, *A perpetua ricordanza di Riccardo Pacifici*, Comunità israelitica di Genova, Genova 5728-1967.
A. Milano, *Immagini del passato ebraico, Comunità Ligure*, RMI, Roma 1974.
G.G. Musso, *Per la storia degli ebrei in Genova nella seconda metà del Cinquecento. Le vicende genovesi di R. Yosef Hakohen*, in D. Carpi, A. Milano, A. Rofé (a c. di), *Scritti in memoria di Leone Carpi*, Fondazione Sally Mayer, Milano - Gerusalemme 1967, 101-111.
E. Pacifici (a c. di), *Commemorazione di Riccardo Pacifici*, Genova 1984.

Lombardy Region

Aa.Vv., *La scuola ebraica di Milano. Lineamenti di storia e di vita.* Giuntina, Firenze 1956.
G. Albini, *La comunità ebraica in Crema nel secolo XV e le origini del Monte di Pietà*, in «Nuova rivista storica», 65 (1975), 378-406.
A. Antoniazzi Villa, *Un processo contro gli ebrei nella Milano del 1488. Crescita e declino della comunità ebraica lombarda alla fine del Medioevo*, Cappelli, Bologna 1985.
D. Bergamaschi, *Gli ebrei a Cremona*, Monza 1906.
I. Carnevali, *Il ghetto di Mantova*, Forni, Bologna 1975 (rist. anast.).
L. Cavatorta, *La sinagoga israelitica*, in Aa.Vv., *Inventario dei luoghi di culto del viadanese*, I, Castello, Viadana s.a., 49-52.
J. Colombo, *Il problema scolastico per gli ebrei d'Italia nel 1938. La scuola di Milano*, in RMI, 31 (1965), 6, 259-272.
V. Colorni, *Judaica minora*, Giuffré, Milano 1983.
M. Cremascoli, *Il ghetto e gli ebrei di Lodi*, in «Israel», 42 (1957), 21, 3.
D. Di Vita, *Gli ebrei a Milano sotto l'occupazione nazista*, in «Quaderni del centro di studi sulla deportazione e l'internamento», 6, 1969-71.
M. D'Urbino - E. Gentili Tedeschi - A. Rimini, *La ricostruzione del tempio illustrata dai progettisti*, in «Bollettino della comunità israelitica di Milano», 8 (1950), 2, 6.
R. Elia, *La scuola ebraica di Milano*, Comunità israelitica di Milano, Milano 1956.
G. Ferri Piccaluga, *Economia, devozione e politica: immagini di francescani,*

amadeiti ed ebrei nel secolo XV, in AA.VV., *Il Francescanesimo in Lombardia. Storia e arte*, Silvana Editoriale, Milano 1983, 107-122.

P.F. FUMAGALLI, *Tipografia ebraica a Cremona 1556-1576*, Istituto Poligrafico e Zecca dello Stato, Roma 1985.

La posa della prima pietra del ricostruendo tempio, in «Bollettino della comunità israelitica di Milano», 9 (1951), 1, 7.

E. LEVI, *Episodi di vita ebraica milanese fra le due guerre mondiali*, in D. Carpi, A. Milano, A. Rofé (a c. di), *Scritti in memoria di Leone Carpi*, Fondazione Sally Mayer, Milano-Gerusalemme 1967, 229-240.

G. LOPEZ, *Gli ebrei in Lombardia nel Quattro e Cinquecento*, in «Banca popolare di Milano», 14 (1983), 69, 6-13.

ID., *La scuola ebraica dall'emancipazione all'autocoscienza*, in N. RAPONI (a c. di), *Scuola e Resistenza*, La Pilotta, Parma 1978, 97-103.

ID., *Un tempio da «sciori»*, in «Shalom», 14 (1980), 4, 20-21.

A. LUZZATTO - L. MORTARA OTTOLENGHI, *Hebraica Ambrosiana*, Milano 1972.

E. MARANI, *Vie e piazze di Mantova (Analisi di un centro storico)*, in «Civiltà mantovana», 1968, 13, 53-59.

A. MILANO, *Immagini del passato ebraico, Mantova e il Mantovano*, RMI, Roma 1974.

G. REGONINI, *Gli ebrei in Ostiano*, s.l. né a.

A. SACERDOTI, *L'ultimo esame. La mitica via Eupili di Milano*, in «Shalom», 18 (1984), 2, 20-21.

A. SARANO, *Demografia di Milano ebraica negli ultimi cento anni*, in «Bollettino della comunità israelitica di Milano», 10 (1952), 3, 5.

ID., *Sette anni di vita ed opere della comunità israelitica di Milano* (aprile 1945 - maggio 1952), «Bollettino della comunità israelitica di Milano», Milano 1952.

R. SEGRE, *Gli ebrei lombardi nell'età spagnola. Storia di una espulsione*, Accademia della Scienze, Torino 1973.

S. SHAERF, *Appunti storici sugli ebrei della Lombardia*, in RMI, 2 (1926), 1-2, 33-49.

S. SIMONSOHN, *History of the Jews in the Duchy of Mantua*, Jerusalem 1977.

ID., *The Jews in the Duchy of Milan*, Jerusalem 1982.

Veneto Region

P. ALAZRAKI - M.G. SANDRI, *Arte e vita ebraica a Venezia (1516-1797)*, Sansoni, Firenze 1971.

C. BOCCATO, *Il ghetto, oggi: polo dimenticato della storia economica della città*, in «Rassegna economica del Polesine», 1984, 3.

ID. (a c. di), *L'antico cimitero ebraico di San Nicolò di Lido a Venezia*, Comitato per il centro storico ebraico di Venezia, Venezia 1980.

R. CALIMANI, *Storia del ghetto di Venezia*, Rusconi, Milano 1985.

G. CARLETTO, *Il Ghetto veneziano nel '700 attraverso i catastici*, Carucci, Roma 1981.

D. CASSUTO, *Ricerche sulle cinque sinagoghe (scuole) di Venezia*, Ministero degli esteri, Gerusalemme s.a.

R. CESSI, *Gli ebrei e il commercio della lana in Rovigo nel secolo 18°*, Padova 1906.

G. CHIUPPANI, *Gli ebrei a Bassano*, Pozzato, Bassano 1907.

A. CISCATO, *Gli ebrei a Padova (1300-1800)*, Forni, Bologna 1967 (rist. anast.).

U. FORTIS, *Ebrei e sinagoghe*, Storti, Venezia 1973.

Id. (a c. di), *Venezia ebraica. Atti delle prime giornate di studio sull'ebraismo veneziano (Venezia 1976-1980)*, Carucci, Roma 1982.
U. Fortis - P. Zolli, *La parlata giudeo-veneziana*, Carucci, Roma 1979.
F. Luzzatto, *La comunità ebraica di Conegliano Veneto e i suoi monumenti*, in RMI, 12 (1956), 1, 34-43; 2, 72-80; 3, 115-125; 4, 178-186; 5, 227-238; 6, 270-276; 7, 313-321; 8, 345-360.
Id., *La comunità ebraica di Rovigo*, in RMI, 6 (1932), 11-12, 509-526.
A. Milano, *Immagini del passato ebraico, Comunità Venete*, RMI, Roma 1974.
A. Ottolenghi - R. Pacifici, *L'antico cimitero ebraico di San Nicolò di Lido*, in «Rivista della città di Venezia», 7 (1929), 6.
N. Pavoncello, *Gli ebrei in Verona dalle origini al secolo XX*, Vita veronese, Verona 1960.
Id., *Il tempio israelitico (di Verona). Le guide spirituali e i maestri della comunità israelitica di Verona*, Vita veronese, Verona 1957.
Id., *Le epigrafi dell'antico cimitero ebraico di Treviso*, in RMI, 34 (1968), 4, 221-232.
S.G. Radzik, *Portobuffolè*, Giuntina, Firenze 1985.
G. Reinisch Sullam, *Il ghetto di Venezia, le sinagoghe e il museo*, Carucci, Roma 1985.
C. Roth, *Gli ebrei in Venezia*, Cremonese, Roma 1933.
Id., *La festa per l'istituzione del Ghetto di Verona*, in RMI, 3 (1927), 1, 33-39.
A. Sacerdoti, *E se il ghetto diventasse una università?*, in «Jesus», 6 (1984), 1, 18-21.
E. Tranchini, *Gli ebrei a Vittorio Veneto dal XV al XX secolo*, De Bastiani, Vittorio Veneto 1979.
G. Visentin, *Il ghetto di Padova*, Gregoriana, Padova 1984.

Trentino - Alto Adige Region

N. Caldera, *San Simonino titolo usurpato in cinque secoli di antisemitismo*, in «Letture trentine e altoatesine», 7 (1985), 42-43.
O. Ceretti, *Fecero una strage per inventare un santo*, in «Historia», 21 (1977), 235, 63-67.
R. Francescotti, *Gente di quartiere*, Innocenti, Trento 1980, 91-93.
G. Laras, *La scomunica: note di diritto penale ebraico*, in RMI, 29 (1963), 10, 446-450; 11, 491-496.
F. Steinhaus, *I sopravvissuti*, in «Letture trentine e altoatesine», 7 (1985), 41-42, 63-70.
G. Volli, *Gli ebrei a Riva del Garda*, in Y. Colombo, U. Nahon, G. Romano (a c. di), *Volume speciale in memoria di Attilio Milano*, in RMI, 36 (1970), 7-9, 473-488.
E. Tessandri, *L'Arpa di David*, Campironi, Milano 1967.

Friuli - Venezia Giulia Region

L. Buda - G. Cervani, *La comunità israelitica di Trieste nel secolo XVIII*, Del Bianco, Udine 1983.
S.P. Colbi, *Note di storia ebraica a Trieste nei secoli XVIII e XIX*, in Aa.Vv., *Volume speciale in memoria di Attilio Milano*, in RMI, 36 (1970), 7-9, 59-74.
R. Curiel, *Le origini del ghetto di Trieste*, in RMI, 6 (1932), 9-10, 446-472.

ID., *Gli ebrei di Trieste nel secolo XVIII*, in AA.VV., *Scritti in onore di Dante Lattes*, in RMI, 16 (1938), 237-255.

S. CUSIN, *Antiche sinagoghe triestine*, in *Comunità religiose di Trieste: contributi di conoscenza, a cura dei Civici musei di storia e arte di Trieste*, Istituto per l'inciclopedia del Friuli-Venezia Giulia, Udine 1979.

M. DEL BIANCO COTROZZI, *La comunità ebraica di Gradisca d'Isonzo*, Del Bianco, Udine 1983.

G. DONATI (a c. di), *Ebrei in Italia: deportazione, resistenza*, Cdec, Giuntina, Firenze 1975.

P.C. IOLY ZORATTINI, *Insediamenti ebraici*, in T. Miotti (a c. di), *Castelli del Friuli*, VI, *La vita nei castelli friulani*, Del Bianco, Udine 1981, 125-145.

ID., *Aspetti e problemi dei nuclei ebraici in Friuli durante la dominazione veneziana*, in AA.VV., *Venezia e la terraferma attraverso le relazioni dei rettori*, Giuffré, Milano 1981, 227-236.

ID., *I cimiteri ebraici del Friuli veneto*, in «Studi veneziani», 1984, n.s. VIII, 375-390.

ID., *Gli insediamenti ebraici nel Friuli veneto e la ricondotta del 1777*, in «Archivio Veneto», serie V, 121 (1983), 5, 23.

ID., *Gli ebrei a Chiavris: cinque secoli di storia*, in «Memorie storiche Forogiuliesi», 1981, LXI, 87-97.

ID., *Il prestito ebraico nella fortezza di Palma nel secolo XVII*, in «Studi storici Luigi Simeoni», 1983, XXXIII, 271-276.

ID., *L'università degli ebrei di S. Vito al Tagliamento e il suo antico cimitero*, in AA.VV., *Studi forogiuliesi in onore di C.G. Mor*, Deputazione di storia patria per il Friuli, Udine 1983, 223-238.

ID., *Gli ebrei a Udine dal Trecento ai nostri giorni*, in Atti dell'Accademia di Scienze Lettere e Arti di Udine, 1981, LXXIV, 45-58.

ID., *I cimiteri ebraici di Udine*, in «Memorie storiche Forogiuliesi», 1982, LXII, 45-60.

ID., *Gli ebrei a Spilimbergo*, in «Splimbèrc», Società filologica friulana, 1984, 137-140.

ID. (a c. di), *Gli ebrei a Gorizia e a Trieste tra «ancien régime» ed emancipazione*, Del Bianco, Udine 1984.

P.C. IOLY ZORATTINI - G. TAMANI - A. VIVIAN, *Judaica forojuliensia*, Studi e ricerche sull'ebraismo del Friuli-Venezia Giulia, I, Doretti, Udine 1984.

F. LUZZATTO, *Cronache storiche della università degli ebrei di San Daniele del Friuli. Cenni sulla storia degli ebrei del Friuli*, in RMI, 30 (1964).

A. MILANO, *Immagini del passato ebraico, Comunità Venete*, RMI, Roma 1974.

P. NISSIM, *Intorno alle vecchie sinagoghe di Trieste*, in RMI, 26 (1960), 7, 329-346.

A. SCOCCHI, *Gli ebrei di Trieste nel Risorgimento italiano*, Libreria mazziniana, Trieste 1952.

M. STOCK, *Nel segno di Geremia. Storia della comunità israelitica di Trieste dal 1200,* Istituto per l'enciclopedia del Friuli-Venezia Giulia, Udine 1979.

Emilia Romagna Region

E. ARTOM, *I portoni del ghetto*, in RMI, 16 (1950), 10, 291-309.

A. BALLETTI, *Gli ebrei e gli estensi*, Forni, Bologna 1969 (rist. anast.).

G. BASSANI, *Il giardino dei Finzi Contini*, Einaudi, Torino 1971.

ID., *Cinque storie ferraresi*, Einaudi, Torino 1956.

M. Cassoli, *Carpi. Gli uomini e le opere nel tempo*, Mutilati, Carpi 1973.
B. Colombi, *Museo ebraico di Soragna*, in «Bollettino della comunità israelitica di Milano», 39 (1982), 12, 7.
R. Finzi, *Correggio nella storia e nei suoi figli*, Arca, Correggio 1983.
L. Leoni, *Le comunità che scompaiono. Cento*, in «Israel», 17 (1931), 11, 5.
Id., *Le comunità che scompaiono. Lugo*, in «Israel», 17 (1931), 14, 9.
F. Levi, *Le comunità ebraiche negli stati parmensi*, in «Ha-tikwà», 34 (1982), 222, 5.
G. Lopez, *Il sefer in vetrina*, in «Shalom», 16 (1982), 10, 30-31.
I.M. Marach, *Presenza ebraica a Lugo*, in «In Rumâgna», 1985.
A. Milano, *Immagini del passato ebraico, Comunità Emiliane e Romagnole*, RMI, Roma 1974.
Id., *Documento sui banchieri ebrei a Modena*, in RMI, 11 (1937), 10, 450-455.
G Muggia, *Un verso di un salmo biblico sopra un antico palazzo di Bologna*, Bologna 1964.
U. Nahon, *Scandiano*, in Id., *Glorie del passato e luci d'avvenire dell'Italia ebraica*, in «Israel», 44 (1959), 28, 5.
Id., *Il tempio di Reggio Emilia. Note di storia e di cronaca*, in «Israel», 44 (1958), 11, 5; 12-13, 7.
A.J.M. Pacifici, *A Cortemaggiore, più di 50 anni fa*, in Y. Colombo, U. Nahon, G. Romano (a c. di), *Volume speciale in memoria di Attilio Milano*, in RMI, 36 (1970), 7-9, 238-288.
L. Padoa, *Storia di una piccola comunità ebraica: Scandiano*, Comune di Scandiano, 1985.
R. Passeri, *La banca medioevale di Oliveto*, in «Samodia», 2 (1978-79), 45-50.
A. Pesaro, *Memorie storiche sulla comunità ferrarese*, Forni, Bologna 1967 (rist. anast.).
O. Rombaldi, *Correggio. Città e principato*, Banca popolare di Modena, Modena 1979.
Id., *Storia di Novellara*, AGE, Reggio Emilia 1967.
M. Rossi, *Guida di Lugo*, Lugo 1925.
I. Vaccari, *Villa Emma. Un episodio agli albori della Resistenza Modenese nel quadro delle persecuzioni razziali*, in «Quaderni dell'Istituto storico della Resistenza in Modena e Provincia», 1, 1960.
G. Volli, *Gli ebrei a Lugo*, in «Studi lughesi», I, 1970.
Id., *Il caso Mortara nel primo centenario*, RMI, Roma 1960.
Id., *La comunità di Cento e un suo documento inedito del 1776*, in RMI, 17 (1951), 5, 205-209.

Tuscany Region

Aa.Vv., *Discorsi per l'inaugurazione del Museo ebraico di Firenze*, Giuntina, Firenze 1982.
Aa.Vv., *Atti del convegno «Il centenario del Tempio israelitico di Firenze»*, Giuntina, Firenze 1985.
Aa.Vv., *Atti del convegno di Livorno 6-7 marzo 1984*, in RMI, 50 (1984), 9-12, 479-862.
A.N.V., *Il giglio di Davide*, in «Shalom», 16 (1982), 10, 32.
G. Carocci, *Il ghetto di Firenze e i suoi ricordi*, Forni, Bologna 1978 (rist. anast.).
U. Cassuto, *Gli ebrei a Firenze nell'età del Rinascimento*, Olschki, Firenze 1965.
S. Fei, *Firenze 1881-1898: la grande operazione urbanistica*, Officina, Roma 1977.

G. Laras, *La compagnia per il riscatto degli schiavi di Livorno*, in Aa.Vv., *Scritti in memoria di Paolo Nissim*, in RMI, 38 (1972), 7-8, 87-130.
Id., *I marrani di Livorno e l'Inquisizione*, in Aa.Vv., *Atti del Convegno «Livorno e il Mediterraneo nell'età medicea»*, Bastogi, Livorno 1978.
Lettere da Monte San Savino, in «Shalom», 13 (1979), 8, 17-20.
M. Luzzati, *L'insediamento ebraico a Pisa*, in *Livorno e Pisa: due città e un territorio nella politica dei Medici*, Nistri-Lischi e Pacini, Pisa 1980.
Id., *Antichi cimiteri ebraici a Pisa*, in *Gli ebrei in Toscana dal Medioevo al Risorgimento*, Olschki, Firenze 1980.
Id., *La casa dell'ebreo*, Nistri-Lischi, Pisa 1985.
A. Milano, *Immagini del passato ebraico, Comunità Toscane*, RMI, Roma 1974.
U. Nahon, Pitigliano, in Id., *Glorie del passato e luci d'avvenire dell'Italia ebraica*, in «Israel», 44 (1959), 26, 3.
N. Pavoncello, *Notizie storiche sulla comunità ebraica di Siena e la sua sinagoga*, in Y. Colombo, U. Nahon, G. Romano (a c. di), *Volume speciale in memoria di Attilio Milano*, in RMI, 36 (1970), 7-9, 289-314.
G. Romano, *La nuova sinagoga di Livorno*, in «Quaderni della Labronica», 10, s.a., 5-16.
A. Sacerdoti, *A pranzo dalla signora Bassani*, in «Shalom», 16 (1982), 8, 22-24.
S. Servi, *Anatomia di una comunità italiana/1*, in «Alef Dac», 1984, 21, 5-10.
S.A. Toaff, *Cenni storici sulla comunità ebraica e sulla sinagoga di Livorno*, in RMI, 21 (1955), 9, 411-426.
Id., *Livorno, comunità sefardita*, in Aa.Vv., *Scritti in memoria di Paolo Nissim*, in RMI, 38 (1972), 7-8, 203-209.

Marche Region

G. Disegni, *Pesaro, Urbino, Senigallia, Ancona*, in «Ha-keillah», 7 (1982), 5, 4.
R. Elia, *Ricordi del tempio di Ancona*, in Aa.Vv., *Scritti in memoria di Guido Bedarida*, Giuntina, Firenze 1966, 71-76.
G. Laras, *Il cimitero ebraico di Monte Cardeto ad Ancona*, in RMI, 29 (1963), 3-4, 154-157.
Id., *Notizie storiche e prammatiche degli ebrei di Ancona nel sec. XVIII*, in Aa.Vv., *Scritti in memoria di Guido Bedarida*, Giuntina, Firenze 1966, 87-98.
Id., *Una «sommossa» nel ghetto di Ancona sul finire del secolo XVIII*, in E.M. Artom, L. Caro, S.J. Sierra (a c. di), *Miscellanea di studi in memoria di Dario Disegni*, Scuola Rabbinica Marguleis - Disegni, Torino 1969, 123-138.
Id., *Un censimento degli ebrei di Ancona del 1807*, in «Rivista italiana di studi napoleonici», 19 (1982), 1-2, 187-200.
A. Milano, *Immagini del passato ebraico, Comunità Marchigiane*, RMI, Roma 1974.
E. Moscati, *L'università israelitica di Urbino*, in «Ha-tikwà», 34 (1982), 221, 6-7.
M.L. Moscati, *La sinagoga ritrovata*, in «Bollettino della comunità israelitica di Milano», 42 (1985), 10, 11.
U. Nahon, *Pesaro, Urbino*, in Id., *Glorie del passato e luci d'avvenire dell'Italia ebraica*, in «Israel», 44 (1959), 25, 3.
Id., *Ancona*, in Id., ivi..., 44 (1959), 28,5.
S. Saffiotti Bernardi, *Gli Ebrei e le Marche nei secc. XIV-XVI: bilancio di studi, prospettive di ricerca*, in Aa.Vv., *Aspetti e problemi della presenza ebraica nell'Italia centro-settentrionale (secoli XIV e XV)*, in «Quaderni dell'Istituto di scienze storiche dell'università di Roma», 1983, 2, 227-272.

S. Sierra, *Il sacco del ghetto di Senigallia nel 1799 in un documento dell'epoca*, in Y. Colombo, U. Nahon, G. Romano (a c. di), *Volume speciale in memoria di Attilio Milano*, in RMI, 36 (1970), 7-9, 381-388.
A. Toaff, *Commercio del denaro ed ebrei romani a Terni* (1296-1299), in Aa.Vv., *Annuario di studi ebraici '80-'84*, Carucci, Roma 1984.

Lazio Region

Aa.Vv., *Il ghetto, struttura differenziata nel tessuto del centro storico di Roma*, Kappa, Roma 1975.
Aa.Vv., *Roma ebraica nel 5707*, Sabbadini, Roma 1946.
U. Fortis, *Ebrei e sinagoghe*, Storti, Venezia 1973.
R.L. Geller e H. Geller, *Roma ebraica. Duemila anni di immagini*, Viella, Roma 1983.
A. Milano, *Immagini del passato ebraico, Roma e la Campagna Romana*, RMI, Roma 1974.
Id., *Sugli Ebrei a Viterbo*, in Aa.Vv., *Scritti sull'Ebraismo in memoria di Guido Bedarida*, Giuntina, Firenze 1966, 137-150.
Id., *Ricerche sulle condizioni economiche degli ebrei a Roma (1555-1848)*, in RMI, 5 (1930), 9, 445-465; 10-11, 545-566; 12, 629-650; 6 (1931), 1-2, 52-73; 3-4, 159-168.
Id., *Il ghetto di Roma. Illustrazioni storiche*, Staderini, Roma 1964.
N. Nahon, *La nuova scuola di Roma*, in Id., *Glorie del passato e luci d'avvenire dell'Italia ebraica*, in «Israel», 44 (1959), 28, 5.
N. Pavoncello, *Le comunità ebraiche laziali prima del bando di Pio V*, in Aa.Vv., *Lunario Romano 1980: Rinascimento nel Lazio*, Palombi, Roma 1979, 47-77.
Id., *Antiche sinagoghe in Roma*, in «Lazio ieri e oggi», 18 (1982), 3, 68-70.
Id., *Ricordi di ebrei a Genazzano*, in «Lazio ieri e oggi», 16 (1980), 12, 288-290.
Id., *Ricordi di ebrei in Ariccia*, in «Castelli romani», 25 (1980), 7, 105-107.
Id., *Ricordi di ebrei in Velletri*, in RMI, 39 (1973), 6, 359-368.
Id., *Gli ebrei negli statuti di Cori*, in RMI, 46 (1980), 5-8, 165-172.
E.F. Sabatello, *Aspetti economici ed ecologici dell'ebraismo romano prima, durante e dopo le leggi razziali (1928-1965)*, in D. Carpi, A. Milano, U. Nahon (a c. di), *Scritti in memoria di Enzo Sereni*, Fondazione Sally Mayer, Milano-Gerusalemme 1970, 254-292.
A. Sacerdoti, *Tredici sinagoghe per gli ebrei*, in «Jesus», 8 (1986), 1, 426-429.
G. Segre, *Cinque scole un tempio. La storia del ghetto di Roma*, in «Ha-tikwà», 33 (1981), 217, 7.
E. Toaff, *Il carnevale di Roma e gli Ebrei*, in U. Nahon (a c. di), *Scritti in memoria di Sally Mayer*, Fondazione Sally Mayer, Milano-Gerusalemme 1956, 325-343.
S. Waagenaar, *Il ghetto sul Tevere. Storia degli Ebrei di Roma*, Mondadori, Milano 1972.

Abruzzo, Campania, Puglia, Calabria, Sicily & Sardinia Region

G. Bedarida, *Gli ebrei di Sardegna*, in RMI, 11 (1936), 8-9, 328-358; 10, 424-443.

V. Bonazzoli, *Gli ebrei del regno di Napoli all'epoca della loro espulsione*, in «Archivio storico italiano», 1981, 508, 179-288.

P. Capobianco, *Gli ebrei a Gaeta*, La Poligrafica, Gaeta 1981.

G. Cividalli, *Ritorno a San Nicandro*, in RMI, 34 (1973), 4, 226-236.

C. Colafemmina - P. Corsi - G. Dibenedetto (a c. di), *La presenza ebraica in Puglia*, Fonti documentarie e bibliografiche, Archivio di Stato di Bari, Bari, s.a.

C. Colafemmina, *Gli ebrei a Manduria*, in «Cenacolo», 7 (1977).

Id., *«La «giudea» di Castellaneta*, in «Cenacolo», 9 (1979), 17-25.

D. Colombo, *Ritorno a San Nicandro*, in RMI, 38 (1972), 9, 442-448.

R. Cotroneo, *Gli ebrei della Giudecca di Reggio Calabria*, in «Rivista storica calabrese», 1908, 11-12.

G. de Antonellis, *Le quattro giornate di Napoli*, Bompiani, Milano 1973.

I. Di Nepi, *L'ebreo che fa fiorire gli alberi. ...gli ebrei in Sardegna*, in «Shalom», 16 (1982), 11, 24.

O. Dito, *La storia calabrese e la dimora degli ebrei in Calabria dal secolo V alla seconda metà del secolo XVI*, Brenner, Cosenza 1979.

N. Ferorelli, *Gli ebrei nell'Italia meridionale dall'età romana al secolo XVIII*, Forni, Bologna 1966 (rist. anast.).

S. Foa, *Ebrei e Sardegna*, in «Israel», 42 (1957), 47, 6.

G. Franchetti, *Ebrei di Calabria*, in «Ha-keillah», 44 (1984), 3, 16.

M. Gaudosio, *La comunità ebraica di Catania nei secoli XIV e XV*, Catania 1974.

C. Giordano - I. Kahn, *Gli ebrei in Pompei, in Ercolano e nelle città della Campania Felix*, Sicignano, Pompei 1968.

V. Giura, *Storie di minoranze. Ebrei, greci e albanesi nel regno di Napoli*, ESI, Napoli 1984.

G. Infranca, *La Giudecca di Trapani*, Gervasi Modica, Trapani, s.a.

I. La Lumia, *Gli ebrei siciliani*, Sellerio, Palermo 1984.

P.E. Lapide, *Mosè in Puglia*, Longanesi, Milano 1958.

C. Medina, *Tracce di marranesimo in Sardegna*, in RMI, 10 (1935), 2-3, 145-146.

A. Messina, *Le comunità ebraiche della Sicilia nella documentazione archeologica*, in «Henoch», 3 (1981), 2, 200-219.

A. Milano, *Immagini del passato ebraico, Italia meridionale*, RMI, Roma 1974.

Id., *Vicende economiche degli Ebrei nell'Italia meridionale durante il Medioevo*, in RMI, 20 (1954), 3, 76-89; 4, 110-122; 5, 155-174; 6, 217-222; 7, 276-281; 8, 322-331; 9, 372-384; 10, 433-441.

Id., *La consistenza numerica degli Ebrei della Sicilia al momento della loro cacciata*, in RMI, 20 (1954), 1-2, 16-24.

N. Pavoncello, *Gli ebrei in Sicilia*, in «Israel», 5 (1966), 13, 7.

I. Sacerdote, *Il centenario della comunità di Napoli*, in RMI, 31 (1965), 2, 90-96.

A. Varone, *Presenze giudaiche e cristiane a Pompei*, D'Auria, Napoli 1978.

PHOTOGRAPHIC CREDITS

The publishing houses involved in the publication of this book would like to thank the following people for their photographic material: Turin Archive of Jewish Tradition and Customs (photo by Giorio Avigdor); Astifoto; State Library of Cremona; Christiane Bohme; Enzo Bruno; Enzo Cavaglion; Ort Center (photo by Dino Facchia); Circolo il Pergolato of Ferrara and Piero Stefani; Paolo De Benedetti; Luca Fiorentino; Ernesto Franco; Aurelio Heger; Pier Cesare Ioly Zorattini; Ard and Heryk Geller; Oscar Israelowitz; Fasto Levi; Marco Levi; Stella Levi; Guido Lopez; Laura Luzzatto; Paolo Mattioni; Esther Moscati; Mario Novati; Silvio Norzi; Olivetti-Corporate Image (photo by Gianni Berengo Gardin); Emanuele Pacifici; Pro Loco of Soncino; Andrea Ricci; Antonio Roganti; Superintendent of Calabria; Federico Steinhaus; Mario Stock; Gionata Tedeschi; Vittorio Tedeschi; Giorgio Visentin; Irene Lewitt and David Harris, from the Israel Museum and Dr. S. U. Nahon, "Dvir" of Tel Aviv.

JEWISH POPULATION DATA

Ancona............................400
Bologna...........................230
Casale Monferrato..........20
Ferrara............................100
Florence.......................... 1,200
Genoa..............................650
Livorno........................... 750
Mantua...........................140
Merano...........................50
Milan...............................9,500
Modena........................... 114
Naples............................300
Padua.............................200
Parma.............................30
Pisa................................185
Rome..............................15,000
Turin..............................1,300
Trieste............................1,050
Venice............................630
Vercelli...........................50
Verona............................100

CATALOG

UNITED STATES JEWISH TRAVEL GUIDE (5th Edition)
by Oscar Israelowitz
660 pages ISBN 1-878741-40-3 **$24.95** (plus $3.00 shipping)

EAT YOUR WAY THROUGH AMERICA
- A Kosher Dining Guide (5th Edition)
by Oscar Israelowitz
125 pages ISBN 1-878741-41-1 **$9.95** (plus $2.00 shipping)

GUIDE TO JEWISH EUROPE - Western Europe 10th Edition
by Oscar Israelowitz
396 pages ISBN 1-878741-39-X **$19.95** (plus $2.50 shipping)

ITALY JEWISH TRAVEL GUIDE (4th Edition)
by Annie Sacerdoti
242 pages ISBN 1-878741-42-X **$19.95** (plus $2.50 shipping)

ISRAEL TRAVEL GUIDE
by Oscar Israelowitz
350 pages ISBN 1-878741-26-8 **$19.95** (plus $2.50 shipping)

CANADA JEWISH TRAVEL GUIDE
by Oscar Israelowitz
196 pages ISBN 1-878741-10-1 **$9.95** (plus $2.00 shipping)

SYNAGOGUES OF THE UNITED STATES
by Oscar Israelowitz
200 pages (paper) ISBN 1-878741-09-8 **$24.95** (plus $2.50 shipping)
(hard cover) ISBN 1-878741-11-X **$29.95** (plus $3.00 shipping)

GUIDE TO THE JEWISH WEST
by Oscar Israelowitz
320 pages ISBN 1-878741-06-3 **$11.95** (plus $2.00 shipping)

NEW YORK CITY SUBWAY GUIDE
by Oscar Israelowitz
260 pages ISBN 0-961103607-1 **$6.95** (plus $2.50 shipping)

ISRAELOWITZ PUBLISHING
P.O.Box 228 Brooklyn, NY 11229
Tel. (718) 951-7072
E-Mail oscari 477 @aol.com

WELCOME BACK TO BROOKLYN
by Brian Merlis & Oscar Israelowitz
172 pages ISBN 1-878741-14-4 **$19.95** (plus $2.50 shipping)

BROOKLYN - THE WAY IT WAS
by Brian Merlis
250 pages (paper) ISBN 1-878741-20-9 **$24.95** (plus $2.50 shipping)
(hard cover) ISBN 1-878741-21-7 **$39.95** (plus $3.50 shipping)

BROOKLYN - THE CENTENNIAL EDITION
by Brian Merlis
132 pages ISBN 1-878741-33-0 **$19.95** (plus $2.50 shipping)

BROOKLYN'S GOLD COAST - The Sheepshead Bay Communities
by Brian Merlis
160 pages (paper) ISBN 1-878741-49-7 **$19.95** (plus $2.50 shipping)
(hard cover) ISBN 1-878741-48-9 **$24.95** (plus $3.00 shipping)

BOROUGH PARK CENTENNIAL EDITION
by Oscar Israelowitz
96 pages ISBN 1-878741-36-5 **$19.95** (plus $2.50 shipping)

BROOKLYN'S PARK SLOPE - A Photo Essay (1890-1999)
by Brian Merlis
160 pages (hard cover only) ISBN 1-878741-47-0 **$29.95** (+$3.00)

ELLIS ISLAND GUIDE with Lower Manhattan (1998 Edition)
by Oscar Israelowitz
128 pages ISBN 1-878741-01-2 **$7.95** (plus $2.00 shipping)

THE JEWISH HERITAGE TRAIL OF NEW YORK
by Oscar Israelowitz
196 pages ISBN 1-878741-37-3 **$14.95** (plus $2.00 shipping)

LOWER EAST SIDE TOURBOOK (6th Edition)
by Oscar Israelowitz
150 pages ISBN 1-878741-38-1 **$9.95** (plus $2.00 shipping)

U.S. HOLOCAUST MEMORIAL MUSEUM & WASHINGTON, D.C. GUIDE
by Oscar Israelowitz
126 pages ISBN 1-878741-16-0 **$7.95** (plus $2.00 shipping)

GLOSSARY

ADAR. Sixth month in the Hebrew calendar.

ADEI. Association of Jewish Women in Italy. It was founded in Milan in 1927 and is the Italian branch of WIZO (Women's International Zionist Organization).

ALIYAH BET. Clandestine immigration organization which was organized toward the end of the British mandate in Palestine.

APPAM. Abbreviation formed by the Hebrew initials of the cities of Asti, Fossano, and Moncalvo.The special ritual in the synagogue service was introduced by a group of Jews who arrived in these cities after their expulsion from France.

ARON (KODESH). Holy Ark in which the Torahs are stored. The Aron is usually located along the eastern wall of the synagogue, facing Jerusalem.

ASHKENAZ. Pertaining to Jews who lived in the Rhine and spread through central Europe; the term eventually was used to include all Jews who observe the "German" synagogue ritual. The common language spoken by Ashkenazic Jews is Yiddish.

AZZIMO. Unleavened bread, matzoh, used during the Passover holiday.

BIMAH. Platform used during the reading of the Torah. Bimah is the term used in an Ashkenazic congregation.Sephardic Jews call the reading platform, Tevah. Some call it Alememar, from the Arabic, al-minbar.

CALENDAR. The Hebrew calendar is based on the lunar phases. Each month consists of 29 or 30 days, resulting in a year consisting of 353 or 355 days. Every few years, an additional month (leap-month called Adar II) is inserted into the calendar. The Jewish New Year begins in mid-September. The Jewish years are counted from the year 3760 B. C. E. Therefore, 1989 is equivalent to 5749.

CHANUKAH. Eight-day celebration of lights which commemorates the restoration and reconsecration of the Temple in Jerusalem by Judah Maccabaeus in 164 B. C. E.,after it was defiled by Antioch IV of Syria. According to Talmudic legend, the small amount of pure olive oil which Judah Maccabaeus found in the Temple lasted miraculously for eight days. In remembrance of this miracle, eight candles are progressively lit, on eight successive days, on the 8-branched candelabra called the chanukkia or menorah.

CHAYREM. Excommunication which was applied from time to time against localities which were particularly hostile toward the Jews. It also brought with it the prohibition of living there.

CIRCUMCISION. (bris or brit milah) Surgical procedure performed on 8-day-old infant males, as prescribed in the Torah. It is also required for male converts to Judaism.

CROWN OF THE TORAH. (keter or atarah) Silver ornament which surmounts the two rods around which the scroll of the Torah is rolled. Sometimes the two rods end with silver points call rimonim or pomegranates.

DIASPORA. Contrary to popular opinion, the Jewish Diaspora did not begin with the destruction of Jerusalem in the year 70, but began many centuries before. Many Jews left Israel because of commercial reasons. Many were deported to Mesopotamia (north Israel) in 722 B. C. E. and to Judea in 597-86 B. C. E. During the Hellenic Era, Jewish communities were first established in Egypt and then spread the Greek language and culture to many ports throughout the Mediterranean basin.

In the beginning of the Common (Vulgar) Era, the Jewish Diaspora extended well beyond Israel. Many people converted to Judaism during this period.

In the Middle Ages, the Diaspora moved toward Spain, central, and western Europe. In the Late Middle Ages, there was a migration toward eastern Europe. This was due to new trade routes and the pressure of expulsion of the Jews from western regions.

The Jews were expelled from the Iberian peninsula and southern France and moved eastward, mostly through Italy, north Africa and to the Ottoman Empire. Large Jewish centers were created in Greece, Turkey, and Palestine.

From the end of the Middle Ages, Italy hosted Jewish communities coming from the Iberian peninsula, France, and Germany. They joined the older Italian Jewish communities which dated back to Roman times. This explains the presence of diverse rituals and traditions in Italy.

HAGANAH. Jewish self-defense organization founded in Palestine in 1920. This organization ultimately became today's Israel Defense Forces (IDF).

HAGADDAH. The story of the exodus from Egypt which is recited during the seder on Passover eve.

HASHOMER HATZA'IR. Pioneer youth movement with Zionist-socialist philosophy. It was designed to educate the young about life in the kibbutz in Israel. It was organized in Galicia in 1915.

HATIKVAH. Zionist song which later became the National Anthem of Israel. The text was written in 1878 by N. H. Imber and the music by S. Coen.

KOSHER. Term referring to an object (usually food) which is ritually pure, either naturally, or by preparation. The opposite of kosher is *trayf.*

KNESSET. Israeli Parliament, which has its seat in Jerusalem.

KEREN HA-YESOD. Permanent institution which is the financial backbone of the World Zionist Organization. It was founded in London in 1920.

KETUBBAH. Matrimonial contract written in Aramaic and recited during the marriage ceremony. In the Late Middle Ages, as well as in modern times, it was often embellished with splendid miniatures.

JOINT. American Jewish Joint Distribution Committee, founded in 1914 for the release of Jewish war prisoners. It was most active from 1945 to 1952, following the Holocaust. It assisted Holocaust survivors and helped reorganize European Jewish communities which were devastated by the war.

JUS GAZAGA. The judicial code which regulated the rental contract for the houses in the ghettos. These regulations related to the non-Jewish property owners and the Jewish tenants. The Jews were not permitted to be evicted if the property was sold. This right could be transmitted from father to son and was sometimes even sold.

MAGEN DAVID. Star of David. In ancient times, it was a popular decorative sign, without any particular religious significance. In the Middle Ages, it was sometimes called the Seal of Solomon.

In the 18th century, it was found on many ritual objects. By the 19th century, the Star of David became the symbol associated with Judaism. During the Nazi Era, the yellow Star of David was used as a discriminatory symbol for the Jews.

MARRANO. Term used for the Jews of Spain and Portugal from the 15th century who were forced to be baptized, but who secretly remained faithful to the Jewish religion. Many marranos, in order to escape the Inquisition, went overseas to different countries, where they could practice their religion in freedom. They moved to the Ottoman Empire and to the Netherlands.

MENORAH. Candelabra. The seven-branched menorah was one of the holy artifacts used in the Temple in Jerusalem. The menorah appears in ancient catacombs and in the ancient synagogue ruins in Ostia and Bova Marina. It also appears in relief under the Arch of Titus in Rome.

MIKVEH. Ritual bath; an important part of life for Orthodox Jewish women, who must immerse therein as part of the preparation for marriage, and who are required to cleanse themselves in it each month after the menstrual period. The mikveh is also used by converts and for the immersion of dishes and metal pots requiring purification.

MONTHS. The names of the months are of Babylonian origin. The Jewish New Year (Rosh Hashanah) starts in mid-September with the month of Tishre, followed by Cheshvan, Kislev, Tevet, Shvat, Adar, Nissan, Sivan, Iyar, Sivan, Tamuz, Av, and Elul. These months are based on the lunar phases.

MEZUZAH. The right door post is where the rolled-up parchment containing Biblical verses is placed. The Jew kisses the mezuzah as he leaves or enters his house.

MIDRASH. Interpretation of the Scripture.

MILAH. See Circumcision.

PAROCHET. Curtain over the Ark. Many times they are richly ornate cloths portraying traditional motifs such as eagles, lions, crowns, spiraled columns, and vine shoots. The top section is often adorned with a short horizontal garnishing called kapporet. Often, the name of the donor is inscribed on this curtain.

PURIM Jewish holiday which commemorates the salvation of the Jews in Persia from total annihilation. The Scroll of Esther (megilah) is recited in the synagogue. When the name of the wicked Haman is pronounced in the megilah, the children drown-out his name with noise-makers. The holiday also involves the sending of food parcels to neighbors and friends and the giving of charity to the needy. It is customary to dress in costume with masks (similar to the Italian Carnivale) and to drink wine.

RIMONIM. Silver crowns of the Torah.

RITUALS (RITES). All of the rituals in synagogue liturgy can be traced to the Palestinian and Babylonian rites. The German (Ashkenazic) ritual is divided into two groups; Occidental rite (Germany and France), and the Oriental rite (Russia and Poland). These rituals are today found in the Americas, England, and some Italian communities (Piedmont).

The Italian or Roman ritual is closer to the ancient Palestinian rite. It is limited to Italy, Corfu, and a few other communities.

The Sephardic or Spanish ritual draws its roots from the Babylonian rite. It spread to numerous Mediterranean countries, the Netherlands, England, and the Americas after the expulsion of the Jews from the Iberian peninsula. An important branch in the Sephardic ritual is the rite of the Yemenite Jews.

ROSH HASHANAH. Jewish New Year.

SEPHARDIC. Pertaining to the Occidental branch of European Jews settling in Spain, Portugal, and parts of France and Italy. The common language spoken by Sephardic Jews is Ladino, which contains both Spanish and Hebrew words.

SEFER. Book.

SEFER TORAH. Torah

SHALOM. Hello, Good-bye, Peace.

SHAVU'OT. Festival of the Weeks. It is celebrated seven weeks following the onset of Passover. It is also the festival which celebrates the receiving of the Torah on Mount Sinai.

SHOFAR. Ram's horn used during Rosh Hashanah services, the conclusion of Yom Kippur, during fast days, at the end of the month, and for the cheyrem. The shofar will announce the coming of the Messiah.

SYNAGOGUE. Greek term for a place of worship and study. It has also been called Scholo, Scuola, Schule, Shul, etc. In more recent times it has been called temple.

The interior of the synagogue contains the Holy Ark, in which the Torah scrolls are stored. The Ark is usually found along the eastern wall, facing Jerusalem. The reading platform is located in the men's section. The women were usually placed in a secluded gallery above the men's section. The synagogue often has a Hebrew school for the children and a mikveh in the cellar.

Before the Emancipation, the synagogue was built on the top floor of a nondescript building. It did not have any unique exterior façade. The interiors were fashioned after the "style-of-the-period."

This is why some synagogue interiors were designed in the Gothic, Classical, or Moorish styles. They reflected the "period" of the synagogues in Worms, Prague, or Toledo.

Following the Emancipation, congregations built magnificent free-standing synagogue structures in all conceivable idioms, from Classical, Moorish, Eclectic, and even Modern.

SUCCAH. Hut used during the Holiday of Succot, which symbolizes the wandering of the Jews in the wilderness after the exodus from Egypt.

TALMUD. The body of rabbinic discussions, interpretations, and development of the law, already codified in the Mishnah. Its formation extended from the 3rd to 5th century (Talmud Yerushalmi), and from the 3rd to 6th century (Talmud Bavli or Babylonian). The Talmud constitutes the most authoritative expression of the rabbinical tradition.

TALMUD TORAH. Hebrew school.

TASHLICH. Ceremony on the first day of Rosh Hashanah, where the sins of the congregation are symbolically "cast" into the running waters.

TEFILLIN. Phylacteries. Two small leather boxes which contain parchment scrolls with Biblical verses and leather straps. They are worn on a man's head and arm during weekday morning prayer services. Tefillin are worn after the Bar Mitzvah, the age of 13. The custom of wearing Tefillin is mentioned in the Torah.

TEVAH. Reading platform in a Sephardic synagogue.

TORAH. The Bible - Five Books of Moses (Pentateuch).

WIZO. Women's International Zionist Organization, founded in London in 1920. Since 1948, its headquarters was moved to Tel Aviv. The organization provides service to women's education, schools, day care, youth clubs, etc.

INDEX

NOTES

NOTES

NOTES

NOTES

NOTES

NOTES

NOTES

NOTES

NOTES

NOTES

NOTES

NOTES

NOTES

NOTES

NOTES

NOTES